Backstage in a Bureaucracy

Backstage in a Bureaucracy
POLITICS AND PUBLIC SERVICE

Susan M. Chandler and Richard C. Pratt

WITHDRAWN

A Latitude 20 Book
University of Hawai'i Press
Honolulu

Library of Congress Cataloging-in-Publication Data

Chandler, Susan M., 1945–
Backstage in a bureaucracy: politics and public service /
Susan M. Chandler and Richard C. Pratt.
p. cm.
"A Latitude 20 book."
Includes bibliographical references and index.
ISBN 978-0-8248-3501-9 (pbk. : alk. paper)
1. Hawaii. Dept. of Human Services—Management.
2. Hawaii—Social policy.
3. Hawaii—Politics and government—1959–
I. Pratt, Richard, 1941– II. Title.
HV98.H32C43 2011
361.9969068'3—dc22   2010028968

Design and production services provided by
Peak Services (peakservices.squarespace.com)

Printed by Golden Cup Printing Co., Ltd.

Contents

Acknowledgments

Susan Chandler I want to thank Governor Benjamin Cayetano for taking a chance on a political greenhorn (as he liked to call me) and providing me with the opportunity to serve as the director of the Department of Human Services. Deep thanks and appreciation go to Kate Stanley, my deputy director for six and one-half years. Kate's deep understanding of the state's workings and the internal mechanisms of the legislative processes, and her tenacity and perseverance, were invaluable. Her excellent advice, coupled with her skills and good humor, were a tremendous benefit to me and to the progress made at DHS.

This project would not have been completed without the gentle prodding, good ideas, and support of my coauthor, Dick Pratt. The book developed from many chats, many cups of tea, many laughs, and his strong interest in and commitment to improving public organizations and public service leadership. I want to thank my husband, David, who vicariously lived through the peaks and pitfalls of both the directorship of DHS and the writing of this book. His sage advice, additional perspective, and continuous cheerleading were extremely helpful. And finally, I want to thank the staff of the Department of Human Services. My faith and respect for those who work in public service grew over the years I worked there, and their dedication is awesome!

Dick Pratt I want to thank Charlene Young for her thoughtful comments on the early drafts. Charlene was a state deputy director, and for many years she has provided advice and assistance to government and nonprofit organizations. Her willingness to give time to this project reflects her commitment to building effective public organizations.

When Susan Chandler was nearing the end of her time in the director's seat, I asked her if she'd be willing to think about a project like this. Her immediate response was "Yes!" which was a nice surprise given how hard she'd been working for eight years. Her energy, enthusiasm, and passion for public work dissolved the tedium of having to read and reread the manuscript until we almost could recite it from memory. Special thanks to the students in our public service leadership program, many of whom hold demanding positions, for what they've taught me. Wives often are recognized for their patience with spouses who are preoccupied with a writing project. My wife, Debbie, did more than put up with me. She became actively involved with the book in its early stages, reading our drafts and making suggestions for how to bring it to life.

We both want to recognize the contributions of the staff of the University of Hawai'i Press. Bill Hamilton, its director, immediately understood what we were trying to do and then offered a series of suggestions that made it far better than it would have been. We're also impressed by and indebted to the careful work of Pat Matsueda and the people at Peak Services who copyedited, typeset, and designed this book.

List of Abbreviations

AG	Attorney General
B&F	Budget and Finance
BESSD	Benefits, Employment and Support Services Division
CPS	Child Protective Services
DoAG	Department of the Attorney General
DAGS	Department of Accounting and General Services
DBEDT	Department of Budget, Economic Development and Tourism
DHRD	Department of Human Resource Development
DHS	Department of Human Services
DLNR	Department of Land and Natural Resources
DOE	Department of Education
DOH	Department of Health
DOT	Department of Transportation
EBT	Electronic Benefit Transfer
EOA	Executive Office on Aging
FAAC	Financial Assistance Advisory Committee
FEMA	Federal Emergency Management Agency
IVA	Internal Vacancy Announcement
MOU	Memorandum of Understanding
MQD	Medicaid/QUEST Division
NHS	National Health Service
OYS	Office of Youth Services
PHA	Public Housing Authority
QUEST	Quality, Universal, Equity, Service, Transformative (Medicaid program)
SSD	Social Services Division
UH	University of Hawaiʻi
UHM	University of Hawaiʻi at Mānoa
UPW	United Public Workers
VRSBD	Vocational Rehabilitation and Services to the Blind Division

1 | Introduction

The importance of state-level administration is growing in the field of public administration for several reasons. As decentralization of the national government moves to the states, the task of the states to accept, discharge, implement, evaluate, and fund depends heavily on each state's administrative capacities (Bowling and Wright, 1998). As a laboratory of democracy, each state must have the capacity and the leadership to innovate and successfully bring high-quality and effective public services to the citizenry.

Top-level state executives are important actors in the political, policy-making, and organizational processes of state government. Bowling and Wright (1998) note that the agencies they head

- perform a broad array of significant public services;
- participate in a broad range of activities across the politics-administration continuum;
- are active in agenda setting and policy formulation tasks;
- implement policies, procedures, and administrative rules and regulations;
- turn legislative mandates into actions;
- oversee organizational and staff operations;
- develop and manage budgets;
- are responsible for inter-organizational relations and intergovernmental networks; and
- generally influence the effectiveness—or the lack of—agency performance.

As this implies, the directors of government departments or agencies have challenging and complex jobs. The scope of this challenge is of course dependent upon the size of the agency and the issues that arise during the period of a director's appointment. At the same time, no matter what the agency, the director is expected to play a number of demanding and publicly significant roles.

These roles include

- high-level policy adviser as a member of the chief executive's cabinet
- public advocate for the administration, especially for new initiatives and in times of political turmoil and crisis
- principal spokesperson to the legislature for the department
- chief negotiator for the department's needs in relation to other departments
- organizational leader
- department administrator
- budget manager (formulator and/or cutter)
- personnel director
- grievance handler
- flak catcher for just about everything that goes on within and outside the department
- media maven
- the voice of the department to the community
- overall leader for the staff and
- the person who is held responsible.

That public institutions are always in transition, and especially so now, is an additional element that makes being a director challenging. Globally, as well as in the United States, debates about what government agencies *should* be doing, and how they *should* be doing it, permeate public and legislative discussions. These discussions have led to a variety of proposals for reform, all of

Managing the workload.

which mean that the heads of agencies must deal with not only the traditional demands placed on them but also the challenge of managing change.

In 1992, David Osborne and Ted Gaebler shook up the existing and some believed sluggish, unresponsive, rule-bound, rigid, and self-protective, self-serving systems inside public bureaucracies with their book *Reinventing Government: How the Entrepreneurial Spirit Is Transforming the Public Sector.* By the mid-1990s, many states were actively implementing reinvention reforms and staff were becoming familiar with such terms as internal competition, performance based budgeting, steering rather than rowing, benchmarking, and monitoring outcomes rather than measuring processes. Inside most public agencies, there began a constant drumbeat to be more efficient, more businesslike, more responsive, and more accountable…all simultaneously of course. Shortly thereafter, the National Academy of Public Administration published its Priority Issues Task Force Report (Washington, D.C., January 10, 2000). The report defined transformation of governance as the academy's major focus. The three elements most important for this transformation were

(1) the growing complexity of relationships between government and civil society,

(2) the need for greater capacity to manage these relationships, and

(3) shifting national responsibilities, both in the direction of international bodies and systems and in the direction of states, localities, and community-based institutions.

Brudney, Hebert, and Wright (2000) examined the values that senior administrators held toward the goals and objectives of their organizations and contrasted them by the race and gender of the leader. The values are of interest to us, so we have listed them below. In descending order of importance, the values or goals underlying the administrators' approaches were

- organizational leadership
- organizational reputation
- quality
- customer service
- effectiveness
- high morale
- high productivity
- budget stability
- organizational growth.

In 2002, Lester Salamon and Odus Elliott added another dimension to the leadership challenge when they argued that much of what government is commonly believed to do has in fact been done by private and nonprofit organizations. Their book *The Tools of Government* explored the challenges of what they referred to as indirect government: the need for public agencies to get things done through organizations over which they have no formal control. For Salamon and Elliott, the real challenge was not the need to reinvent public organizations, but to recognize these public-private partnerships are complex and require skills to make them work on behalf of the public.

Clearly, senior executives try to function in extremely complex environments that have multiple levels and layers of legislative, executive, and judicial oversight, combined with almost constant media, constituent, and advocacy-group attention. There are many stakeholders both inside and outside of government. While diverse, they all have the belief that they are important to the process of influencing public policy and agency direction. The usual suspects include such traditional stakeholders as business, labor, the press and other media, legislators, nonprofit organizations, community-based organizations, advocates, and constituents. However, senior state executives also need to attend to the concerns and issues of other agency directors, line workers, staff officers, and division administrators. In the state of Hawai'i, there are also special issues and concerns of the Native Hawaiians as well as other ethnic and cultural groups. Depending on the issue, these stakeholders may wield significant influence over agency directors (and the governor). The external environment thus makes demands on public agencies and their directors that are unparalleled in the private sector. Many public officials wish that their job were merely to make a better burger and watch the bottom line, rather than to protect the public interest and improve the quality of life!

The Goal of Our Work

This book describes what it is like to lead a large public agency, using the experience of a cabinet member during the administration of Hawai'i Governor Benjamin Cayetano (1994–2002). Susan Chandler was for these eight years the director of the Department of Human Services (DHS), a state agency with more than two thousand employees and an annual budget of $1.2 billion. Our goal in examining her experience is to share something of the real-world, day-to-day life of being director during these turbulent years. Our hope is that these reflections will be instructive to those who are curious about what happens behind the scenes in public agencies and what their leaders do. We hope this inside look will benefit current and future leaders, those who work with them, and people in our community who seek to understand and improve their community and their government.

Who Are We?

A word about us. Susan Chandler (MSW, University of Hawai'i; Ph.D., University of California at Berkeley) is the director of the College of Social Sciences Public Policy Center at the University of Hawai'i at Mānoa (UHM) and a half-time faculty member of the UHM Public Administration Program. She joined the faculty in 1976. In 1992, she enrolled in a Public Administration Program course taught by Dick Pratt: "Reforming Public Organizations." Her years of frustration as a social-work advocate had spurred her interest in taking this class. Inspired in fall 1993 during a sabbatical leave, she enrolled in the Maxwell School of Citizenship and Public Affairs at Syracuse University, obtaining a certificate in public administration. Just as she was finishing her certificate program, Benjamin Cayetano, then Hawai'i's newly elected governor, asked her to interview for a cabinet post in his administration. She returned from New York, was interviewed and hired, and began her tenure as director of DHS in January 1994.

Dick Pratt (MEd Administration, University of Denver; Ph.D., University of Hawai'i) is a professor who founded and directs the Public Administration Program at UHM. Focusing on Hawai'i and the Asia-Pacific region, the program is dedicated to increasing the capacities of public institutions to serve and the abilities of people in public service to lead. Pratt has a long-time interest in reforms that make public agencies both more effective in meeting their goals and more desirable as places for people to work. He has worked with a variety of public agencies in Hawai'i and elsewhere.

A Caveat

This work, we emphasize, is intended to humanize the people who work at DHS—and other public servants in Hawai'i—not criticize the department or its employees. The reality is that some of the people who are most frustrated and concerned with the way the system works are the people in this agency and others. Many are there because they believe in something or have a public or community calling that can't be satisfied elsewhere. Too often, these same people are caught between the desire to do good work, and the obstacles that prevent them—a recurrent theme in this book.

Our goal is not to find fault with these people, but to speak with understanding and humor to the complexity of the settings, situations, and circumstances (aka the system) in which they try to do their work. It is our shared hope that in highlighting this complexity we also may see opportunities for improvement.

Hawai'i

Before we begin this journey of reflection, some context setting is in order. Hawai'i has a statewide population of just under 1.3 million. Its political system is very likely the most centralized of all fifty states, having evolved from a kingdom to a plantation system whose leaders had little interest in the virtues of local government. In the early days of the territory, after 1900, the heads of government and the plantation businesses were concerned that any local government would lessen their control of a society in which they were decidedly a minority.

The centralized system was reinforced later in the century when some people came to believe this structure could protect the small communities

Governing 1.3 million on seven islands.

in the neighbor islands from the domination of Honolulu. Through the seniority system, neighbor-island legislators could exert significant power in the state legislature. For example, a county system of education based on a county taxing structure (property taxes or bonds) might have resulted in a decidedly unequal distribution of money per child. The strong, centralized Department of Education (DOE) was designed to ensure equality of public education by concentrating power at the state level and by using state, rather than local or bond dollars for support.

This debate continues today. The person who succeeded Governor Cayetano, Linda Lingle, supports multiple, decentralized school districts with significant decision-making power. The Democrat-controlled legislature this Republican governor has to work with favors a student-based budgeting formula that moves money toward the more needy (and thus more costly) student, but keeps the DOE organizational structure pretty much in place. Even in the face of huge state deficits, the centralized structure of a state-run school board remains.

This debate notwithstanding, Hawai'i's state agencies still dominate the landscape and take on functions that in other places are the responsibility of county or municipal governments. Contributing further to Hawai'i's governmental centralization is the relative strength of the governor's office in comparison to that of other states. (For more about this, see *Hawai'i Politics and Government,* a book by Pratt with Zachary Smith.)

One other note about the context. Life as a member of the Cayetano cabinet was strongly influenced by the economic conditions of that period. Governor Cayetano came into office in 1994 and immediately found, to his great surprise, an enormous budget shortfall. Although the press had been reporting the huge spending initiatives being undertaken toward the end of the previous administration, that of Governor John Waihee, and there were plenty of warning signs about the potential for an economic downturn, the speed with

These are very big cuts!

which the deficit grew and the size it attained were shocking. It took months for the new administration to fully understand how much it would have to cut programs and services and what else it would have to do to cope with the new economic reality. The early cabinet meetings only slowly began to focus on the scope of the economic problems ahead. The effect on the Cayetano administration over the next eight years was pervasive. Every department was asked to cut spending again and again. It was a defining issue not only for the governor, but also for the heads of his departments. Chandler's experience would have been different in many ways—internally with her staff and externally with the legislature, the heads of other departments, and public interest groups—if the budget-cutting wolf had not always been at the door.

Book Structure

We have organized these reflections under the major issues faced by a public sector chief executive. These sections are largely in chronological order, beginning with those issues that greet the executive or director when she or he first assumes the office. Beginning with chapter four, each section is preceded by a commentary by Pratt (in italics) placing Chandler's experience in a broader context or relating her points to other issues. We wrote this book after a series of discussions and have tried to keep some of that informal, conversational flavor in the chapters.

We begin with some explanation of why, given the enormous challenges, people serve as directors, and then we provide some background on the department that serves as the case for this study.

2 | What Kind of Person Should Be in These Jobs?

The challenges of heading a government agency are increased by the reality that the vast majority of the people appointed are not prepared by education or experience for many of their new responsibilities. This is a function not only of the difficulty and diversity of a public agency's responsibilities, but also the intricacies of the selection process and the willingness of people to serve. Under the best of circumstances, it would be hard for them to prepare for these diverse duties unless they had come up through the agency's ranks. However, this generally doesn't happen. Appointed individuals usually come to hold high-level positions on the basis of such attributes as a political or personal connection to the governor. These political appointments are made for a variety of reasons, often having as much to do with the person's relationship to the governor (or, in some cases, the president's election campaign) as her capacity to do the job. Of special note here is a survey that revealed only about one-third of top-level state executives had been promoted to agency head from a subordinate position within the agency (Bowling and Wright, 1998). We may assume that very few of those who come to lead and administer agencies as political appointees have administrative experience, especially in the public sector.

Each new administration, in order to advance its own change agenda, wants to bring in a new crop of agency heads. These leaders are expected to have an orientation and perspective supportive of the newly elected administration, as well as the skills to implement its agenda. There clearly are trade-offs. On the one hand, it is easier to come to policy decisions and there are fewer disagreements in public. On the other, important points of view are likely to be excluded. If the like-minded appointees are ideological in nature, that will probably be irritating to civil servants. But civil servants also want some stability at the top. President Ronald Reagan overtly attempted to stock his executive agencies with persons who understood and supported his goals and objectives, who were philosophically sympathetic to his perspectives on government and public sector management. Career professionals in that administration were often seen as the enemy, and attempts were made to exclude them from important policymaking duties and responsibilities. This strategy can have disastrous effects. When Hurricane Katrina hit the Gulf Coast, the politically appointed director of Federal Emergency Management Agency (FEMA), Michael Brown—who had no previous disaster-management experience but was a supporter of President George W. Bush—was severely criticized for being unable to lead. After great outcry, he was axed and returned to the private sector. While the civil service staff does not typically turn over when there is a political change, if the leadership doesn't respect it, include it in decision making, and utilize its expertise, internal disasters may also occur. There is the related question of how much consensus, or dissensus, is desirable in appointments. If the appointees are only people who agree with and are loyal to the chief executive, that may breed unhappiness among the staff members who feel their knowledge and expertise are being ignored. On the other hand, if more independent individuals are appointed—people who expect to speak their minds and who believe the best decisions are informed by debate—agency staff may come to feel that there is too little predictability at the top.

That surfer looks like good management material.

The challenge of finding executive leadership that is both knowledgeable about the agency's work and loyal to a particular political orientation may be difficult to meet. Some public administration theorists/scholars contend that a good leader and manager may come from any field and still be able to transfer those skills to an agency regardless of the area of responsibility. Others contend that the complexity of the large public agencies now requires specialized expertise and that an administrator must be well versed in the work of the agency in order to provide leadership. The bottom line is that the combination of political loyalty and specialized expertise is hard to find.

3 | Organizational Setting

In Hawai'i, the director of DHS oversees an agency that historically has operated all state welfare programs, the food stamp program, public housing, child and adult protection services, vocational rehabilitation, and health insurance programs for the poor. Its mandate is to offer assistance to all people in the state who are unable to provide for themselves. Through its programs, DHS provides shelter, financial assistance, medical assistance, job training, childcare subsidies, and more. Millions of federal and state dollars and contracted services are provided to more than 200,000 beneficiaries.

In fiscal year 2002 (July 1, 2001, to June 30, 2002), DHS was made up of four divisions:

- The Benefits, Employment and Support Services Division (BESSD) was the largest division, employing about 600 people and managing a budget of $350 million.

- The Medicaid/QUEST Division (MQD) oversaw Medicaid payments and services. It had a budget of over $700 million and a staff of about 140 state and contracted employees. It was responsible for the health insurance of about 200,000 Hawai'i citizens.

- The Social Services Division (SSD) had a budget of $75 million and was staffed by about 460 state employees, as well as private contractors.

- The Vocational Rehabilitation and Services to the Blind Division (VRSBD) had a budget of $18 million, of which federal funds comprised 72 percent. It had 165 state employees, as well as private contractors.

All of these programs receive significant federal funding. Medicaid obtains over 50 percent of its funding from federal funds, and food stamps about 85 percent; welfare programs have block grants of about $90 million for cash assistance and training. During the first seven years of the Lingle administration (2003–2010), there was a huge increase in federal awards to the state, and this enlarged the DHS budget substantially. Health insurance eligibility was expanded, and the new director used the infusion of federal funds to expand and privatize child welfare services. The organizational structure of DHS did not change much, however. The new administration altered the personnel structure of the organization by hiring a large number of outside consultants for both program development and administrative services.

DHS also had two administratively attached agencies at the beginning of the Cayetano administration: the Office of Youth Services (OYS), which ran the state's youth correctional facility and provided an array of delinquency prevention services; and the Public Housing Authority (PHA). In 1998, the PHA was transferred to the Department of Budget, Economic Development and Tourism (DBEDT) in an effort to consolidate all housing programs under one agency. In 2003, the legislature decided that all programs for the poor were better coordinated by DHS, and the PHA was returned.

DHS also had five staff offices supporting the divisions and the department: Fiscal Management, Office of Information Technology, Personnel, Management Services, and the Administrative Appeals Office. The staff offices were all located in the Lili'uokalani building in downtown Honolulu, near the state capitol grounds. However, DHS had additional offices spread out across O'ahu and on each island. Some were large (four hundred employees in Kapolei), and others were small, three-person offices, like the one on Lāna'i. The benefits application offices were small units, placed in neighborhoods to be easily accessible and close to where people lived.

With this as background, let's now go backstage in a public bureaucracy.

4 | In the Beginning

Most people may believe that appointment to a high-level government office is a reward for loyal service to the party or the winning candidate. This could be true, but it is unquestionable that the belief political hacks are running our public agencies does nothing to enhance our view of either the agencies or the people in them. Susan Chandler's selection as director and cabinet member, though perhaps unusual and refreshing, raises questions about what kind of knowledge is deemed valuable and what constitutes the appropriate balance between knowledge of any kind—organizational, policy, or professional—and loyalty.

The selection process for a political appointment varies across states and departments. Most governors want to appoint people whom they know, trust, and, often, have worked with before. Many times these people come from the political campaigns of winning candidates. Over the years, however, the role of a director—particularly in large and complex agencies like the department of health, personnel, or human services—has become specialized. Rather than from the political world, human service directors now are frequently hired from other states, other departments, or the private sector to manage these complex agencies.

The Invitation; or, Who Really Gets These Jobs?

Newly elected Hawai'i governor Benjamin Cayetano broke with Island tradition and put job announcements in the local newspapers asking interested (and qualified) people to apply for all of his cabinet posts. To review the applications and conduct interviews, the governor created a ten-member selection committee. The committee that interviewed me included Mazie Hirono, the newly elected lieutenant governor; several of the recently appointed cabinet members, including Margery Bronster, the attorney general (AG), and Earl Anzai, the Budget and Finance (B&F) director; John Radcliffe, an officer of the University of Hawai'i (UH) faculty union; Charles Toguchi, the governor's chief of staff; and a few other advisers and friends of Cayetano.

So, how was the human services director really appointed? I had not been active in the Cayetano gubernatorial campaign or personally acquainted with the governor. Hindsight suggests I was interviewed because the governor had heard about "this lady with a lot of interest and experience in social welfare issues from the University of Hawai'i." Despite the new governor's often-stated ambivalence about the eggheads who came from the university and did not live in the real world, he ended up appointing two cabinet members who were university professors. The other was Seiji Naya, a respected academic economist and researcher, who like me, had had little government experience. Why did he do this?

The governor had spent twelve years in the legislature before becoming the lieutenant governor for eight years and strongly believed that insiders or government bureaucrats often were stuck in their ways. He believed that when he wanted to know *how* to get things done better and quicker, longtime bureaucrats would eloquently explain why they *could not* be done better and quicker. Cayetano felt that academics from the university had access to new knowledge and perhaps would be creative assets to his cabinet. In my case, the appointment was not political in the sense that it was not based upon years of service to the Democratic Party, to Democratic

Maybe we'll find SOMEONE!

candidates, or to the governor. I don't know whether the governor had sought more partisan and politically loyal people, but if he did, none evidently met with his approval (or was willing to take the job). The frequently heard statement among state administrators that a director must be prepared to take the bullet for the governor is unfamiliar to the new appointee, but is quickly learned. In late December 1993, the governor still had not filled the director's position for DHS. All of the other cabinet appointments had been made.

The Interview; or, What Should I Say or Not Say?

While the governor might be the first public servant, on a day-to-day basis he is a person to whom most people, even those with a power base outside of government, are expected to show deference. This presented an interesting problem for Chandler, who comes from an organizational culture (the university) where those norms don't much apply. It also begs the important question of whether it is a good thing—that is, something in the public's interest—for the governor not to hear, on a regular basis, his staff's respectful, but candid, disagreements.

On the one hand, it seems clear that a certain amount of deference is due a governor by the simple fact that his or her authority derives from having been elected by the state's voters. There is also public benefit from decisions being based on a shared and predictable orientation toward issues. On the other hand, discussion and the airing of differences are necessary to avoid group-think-related blunders. And, of course, governors are human and entirely capable of making mistakes. The personalities and experience of those involved will go a long way to determining the right balance in a particular situation, and this is what Chandler had to learn.

As Chandler experienced it, she and the governor connected on shared values and policy priorities. These were enough for the new governor to trust she would do things he agreed with, and served as a kind of stand-in for loyalty.

Reference is made in the following section to the fact that Chandler and her deputy, Kate Stanley, were both haoles *(meaning, in this context, Caucasians) in an agency whose clientele was overwhelmingly Asian and Pacific. It is hard to know what effect this had on the clients or, for that matter, on the staff, also primarily non-Caucasian in a state where no ethnic group has a majority. In this way, Chandler brings up the idea of representative bureaucracy: a public agency as a reflection of the community it serves. The main arguments* for representative bureaucracy are that clients will be better able to identify with people who look like them and that staff members who share their clients' cultural or socio-economic backgrounds will better understand them. This of course soon gets tricky because it may lead to the appointment of people who appear to be the right representatives, but lack needed experience and leadership. Though it is possible to find both in the same person, it is not likely to happen, and a difficult choice may have to be made.

Chandler's comment that salaries and working conditions never came up as a hiring issue for her would be extremely odd in a private sector setting, and more than that, lack of discussion of these matters reflects a serious disadvantage in executive recruitment. Government salaries are set by statute, and usually they are below what a person assuming similar responsibilities in the private sector would make. Therefore, unless people are expecting to make illicit gains for themselves or friends, their primary motivation must be public service. (It is not job security because they will be replaced when whoever appointed them leaves office.) This also means that if new governors are not able to attract competent individuals on the basis of their desire to serve, the public will indeed get what it pays for. In the end, perhaps with the advice of his selection panel, Governor Cayetano chose a greenhorn director primarily on the basis of her educational credentials, recommendations from unknown others, and the values he shared with her.

Chandler's observations in this section also might move us to ask whether it is desirable—and if desirable, possible—to provide new agency heads with a crash course on such matters as leadership, organizational processes, legislative operations, the media, and budgets. It seems like a good idea, yet probably is rarely implemented. This may in part be due to the fact that appointees are typically strong-minded and successful people, even if their professional experience is not in the right areas. It also reflects the reality that, as Chandler discovered, the time needed for this would not be much available after the new job began.

In order to prepare for the job interview for a cabinet-level department head, candidates are given access to the department's "Transition Book." This binder is made up of the department's enabling legislation, budget, programs, and any other information that the previous director thought important. The DHS book was primarily an accounting of the programs, rules, budgets, and staffing patterns of the agency. I found reading it some-

Whoa! I do all this?

what scary and more than a bit intimidating. DHS was clearly a huge and complex organization that seemed to have more acronyms and jargon than everyday words. Would the applicants be quizzed on the transition book's content during the job interview? Who knew?

Early in the interview, it became clear that there seemed to be a connection between the governor and me based on shared values. The governor asked, "What should be done to help the poor and disabled people in Hawai'i, and how should a director of DHS go about providing services to assist them?" The governor made it very clear that he was a kid from Honolulu's hardscrabble neighborhood of Kalihi, that these were the proud people he represented throughout his political career, and that they would always be at the top of his agenda.

During the interview, he posed several challenging and controversial policy questions, which led to some lively and animated discussion. He questioned why people on Hawai'i's Medicaid program could have extensive prescription drug insurance coverage, while other low-income and middle-income people couldn't (including himself). He wanted to know why people eligible for Medicaid benefits got extensive health coverage, yet many people in Hawai'i had no coverage at all. He asked me if I would agree to ration health benefits the way the Medicaid program in Oregon had. On this issue, we had a pretty heated exchange. I knew that Oregon had used its own money (not federal funds) to expand eligibility for the state-run Medicaid program. The state dollars were matched with a significant number of federal dollars. However, Oregon had only rationed those medical procedures considered to be experimental, or those not proven to be medically effective, which was actually a very small number. While the intricacies of the Medicaid program fascinate most policy wonks, they usually produce glazing over of the eyeballs for most people…even some on the search committee listening to our debate. The governor, however, was very engaged.

The members of the interview panel seemed surprised such a vigorous debate was happening in the middle of a job interview. They appeared shocked by the back-and-forth between an applicant for the job and the governor. Several asked me afterwards if I had known the governor before the interview. It later became clear to me that within government, there is a far more deferential mode of communication than is traditional at the university. The governor, trained as an attorney and an active litigator, liked to take on issues head first. While arguing with a governor is perhaps not the usual modus operandi, particularly in a job interview, Cayetano was well known for his feisty behavior and shoot-from-the-hip comments. The daughter of two attorneys, I was quite prepared to actively debate just about any policy issue. Later, I learned that such debates are best held privately and that the norm of cabinet meetings was not to argue with the governor in front of the other directors, and most certainly not in public.

During the interview, the governor asked about my educational background and seemed impressed with "all the academic degrees from fancy places." I remember that he commented several times to the panelists that "this candidate" knew very little about the real world of government and politics and would probably make a lot of mistakes. I later heard that one panel member had asked the governor if he was ready for an academic feminist in the cabinet. Evidently he was.

Surprisingly, the job offer came just two hours after the interview. When the governor called, he said the following, and to me, it seemed like a fabulous job description. "Susan, if you make mistakes trying to do things on behalf of people, I'll back you completely. However, if you make mistakes just to benefit yourself, I'll fire you." I took the job.

The governor suggested Kathleen (Kate) Stanley be the deputy director for DHS. She was very experienced in state government and had served in the legislature and for the previous governor (and in Democratic Party politics) for over thirty years. This turned out to be an excellent way to balance the inexperience of a new director. The governor asked if this would be okay with me, but clearly this was his choice. Unknown to the governor, I had worked with Kate before, at UH, and we had been friends for over thirty years. I couldn't have found a better deputy. She was highly skilled and experienced, and I trusted her completely.

Kate and I laughed when we heard that there was some consternation about the governor hiring two *haole* women as the director and deputy director of DHS. *Haole* is the Hawaiian word that refers to a foreigner or an outsider and today commonly means a Caucasian or white person. Hawaiians, part-Hawaiians, Samoans, and other Pacific Islanders are overrepresented on Hawai'i's welfare rolls and in need of supportive services, so some government people thought it inappropriate, or perhaps insensitive, to have two New Yorkers heading DHS. While both Kate and I had lived in Hawai'i for over twenty-five years, there is a saying in the state that if you didn't graduate from a local high school, you are not local. There is also a subtle, but important, cultural distinction between people who have lived in the islands for a long time, but have not become—and never will be considered—local.

Salary and working conditions never came up in the interview with the governor. Determined by statute and considered public information, salaries are set by the legislature, and the salaries of all directors are the same regardless of department size or responsibilities. The governor frequently expressed appreciation of the dedication of the members of his cabinet who had taken significant salary cuts to enter public service. However, coming into the position as a social work professor, I was the rare appointee who actually received a modest salary increase.

Though it came as quite a surprise to be appointed, I felt that it would be a wonderful opportunity to become active in public life and try to make a difference. Now, after teaching, talking about, reading, and studying policy for years, and becoming a hardened policy wonk, I had the premier job for a person interested in social welfare policy. I was totally committed to social change and believed deeply in public service. I was definitely up for the challenge, but I was also fortunate to have a safety net: a tenured faculty position at the university to return to if things went badly.

The First Week; or, Did It Really Take God Seven Days? That's Reassuring!

Leaping right into the thick of things can be an advantage for a new leader. It permits her to establish authority and a communication style and to quickly build a track record as a person of action. Quick starts also may have significant downsides. Many students of leadership recommend that a new leader spend time getting to know the organization's culture and issues before deciding what to do and how to do it. In a 2007 workshop at UH, David Brubaker recommended not attempting any significant changes for at least two years so that the leader could become thoroughly familiar with the agency's culture. This would include reading through documents and absorbing relevant information, but a wise leader also would find ways to learn the staff's perspective. In Chandler's case, learning the basics of the job and making important organizational decisions coincided. Getting help from people who knew the organization and the system was crucial for her.

Worth noting are her comments on the importance of DHS's physical setting and what the setting conveyed about working there. Bureaucratic offices have a familiar feeling, and it is not a good one. They can convey a no-frills attitude and a seriousness of purpose, but they also can seem lifeless. There is an interesting parallel to public schools, many of which, at least in the past, had this same feeling. Today it is more common to see a multitude of inviting colors on the walls and classroom doors, which educators think contribute to learning. Sprucing up administrative agencies likely would have a similar good effect, but it also might provoke cries of wasting taxpayers' money.

The job began on January 4, 1994, and the first legislative hearing on the department's budget was scheduled for January 10. For a new director, this is a daunting timetable; talk about a steep learning curve. It was of course essential to defer to the senior staffers who had prepared the budget and the budget testimony. It also was vital to quickly learn as much as possible in order to get an understanding of the issues and the internal operations of the department. Another immediate worry was thinking about how to answer legislators' questions about the governor's positions on DHS matters when it wasn't clear what the governor's positions *were*. Does a new director just tell the legislators what he or she thinks? Should she clear positions on controversial issues with the governor? How does she know what is considered controversial?

Deputy Kate Stanley was a huge help. She taught me how to read the state budget, provide successful testimony, schmooze with the important legislators, and navigate the corridors of the capitol building. This included learning how to get in and out without bumping into television crews. Kate, who had been a legislator and had worked in the previous governor's administration as his legislative liaison, clearly knew how government worked. I trusted her political wisdom implicitly.

The first task internally was to select a private secretary. The

TANF   AFDC   DAGS
PWORA   TAONF
    MQD   AAO   BESSD
FAMIS   B&F MSO FMO   LG
    QUEST
SSD   CPS VRSB AG   DHRD

Bureaucratic alphabet soup.

previous administration's acting director was still in the office on my first day. He said, "Hello, hire Ms. H," and then left. That turned out to be terrific advice, and taking it was perhaps the best decision I made in the first six months. My secretary was extremely talented and thoughtful, as well as a skilled organizer and scheduler. She was a valuable asset throughout my entire eight years as director.

The physical setting of the DHS administrative offices is pretty grim. They are located at 1390 Miller Street in downtown Honolulu, across from the Queen's Medical Center. The offices are in a large four-story building shared with the DOE. The director's office was not a friendly place. Most of the offices were overflowing with people, papers, boxes, and cubicles that seemed designed to hide the faces of the staff. All of the offices were painted a sickly green and had unmatched, cast-off furniture. Several employees attempted to display cheery wall hangings and posters, and some left up old holiday decorations made from recycled computer paper or paper clips—anything to add a little color or variety to the workplace. DHS's administrative offices were within walking distance of the capitol, but the physical environment was not a welcoming place for the public or a happy place to work.

A home away from home.

Just Do It!

There are important differences between the staff members who inhabit offices around the central administration and the division administrators spread out across the state. Staff positions are supposed to support the units and individuals who do the real (i.e., direct-service) work of the agency, such as meeting clients or distributing benefits. Staff positions include fiscal and personnel officers, information system technicians, and procurement. When these staff services are giving the line units what they need, the relationships are happy ones. More often than not, though, there is tension between them, and both sides often believe their work is misunderstood. People in staff positions want those in line positions to follow the rules they lay down so that the rules apply to everyone in an orderly and fair way. Those in line positions, by contrast, want their needs better understood or the function decentralized so that they can adapt it to their particular circumstances.

Chandler shares the details of a critical incident that occurred on her first day: a request to sign a Memorandum of Understanding (MOU) between her department and the Department of Health (DOH). Signing it would have had serious repercussions and affected her relations with her staff. She didn't, but it would have been easy given the backlog she had to deal with and how little she knew about the history of this issue. The lesson here is to have a questioning mind at all times—even on the first day, when it is easy to believe that others know how things work and what the right thing to do is.

My first days as director were filled with having to sign literally hundreds of documents. Some were old contracts from the previous administration, and some were documents, letters, and memos from DHS staff that had been waiting for the new director, efficiently and affectionately called the "Dir." Many other documents were difficult to figure out. The advice given to me was, "Just sign." I was at first quite reluctant to sign documents without reading them and fully understanding their importance. To overcome my reluctance, my secretary suggested that I meet the staff officers. This was the first of many fabulous suggestions from her. One by one, the officers came in to see me. Early on, it became apparent that there was tension between the staff officers who were in the same building as the director, and had close access to her, and the division administrators who were spread out all over the island.

The five staff officers headed personnel, management services, information technology, fiscal management, and administrative appeals. They all believed that their offices were severely understaffed, under supported, and less respected than the line divisions, which were much larger and ran the client services and programs. Over the years, budget cuts had taken their toll on the staff offices, and they were accustomed to being the first cut and the last to get new positions. The priority clearly had been to save the line from cuts since they provided direct services to persons in need.

On my desk the first day was an MOU between DOH and DHS. Naively, I thought that a memo between two agencies in the same administration would be a straightforward document designed to improve services to persons who were eligible for programs in both of them. Not exactly. This particular MOU had been a bone of contention for the previous administration, its directors, agency clients, and the legislature. Just signing the MOU would have been an enormous mistake. Fortunately, my very wise secretary alerted me to the fact that this issue was a bit of a bear and suggested that I talk to a few of the division administrators to get some background on it. Since this issue had been around for several years, my secretary, in her capacity as support staff to the previous deputy director, was aware of the interagency controversies and able to provide me with excellent advice.

The complexity of this interagency squabble made it very important, and the squabble still has not been solved—years after I left. The issue focused on persons eligible for Medicaid health care and services because they were mentally challenged or developmentally delayed. DOH, due to its history of administering the Waimano Training School and Hospital on O'ahu, had designed an outpatient program of home and community-based services for this population. These services were funded by Medicaid, which is administered by DHS. The Medicaid eligibility unit is housed and administered by DHS, which is ultimately responsible for program compliance and the expenditure of federal dollars for all eligible persons. Since federal law requires that only one agency in each state be designated as the Medicaid agency, usually the one with the trained eligibility workers and program specialists is responsible for all persons, regardless of their disability. However, DOH had the Developmental Disabilities Branch and an advocacy council designed to ensure that the best services possible were received by persons with developmental disabilities. Thus, DOH wanted control of this program, including the transfer of funds from DHS. Ultimately responsible for the Medicaid program, DHS was reluctant to agree. In the past, there had been instances of DOH spending federal Medicaid dollars that were subsequently disallowed. DHS

> *A DAGS rule (also in statute) requires that each director must sign every contract prior to it being funded. A large agency may have over one thousand contracts a year—some big, some small. In addition, attached to each contract is a statement that the provider is exempt from civil-service rules. This is self-evident since a private provider cannot be part of civil service and therefore has to be exempt. However, the form that the director must sign states the person is indeed exempt from civil service. In fact, there are two forms! One is for the state agency and one for the provider. And each form is then sent to the Department of Human Resource Development for its director's signature.*

was left holding the bag, and on occasion it was required to return already expended federal funds. In addition, DHS believed that services shouldn't be segregated by type of disability and that its staff did an excellent job of matching Medicaid-eligible people with the best and most appropriate services available.

DOH, on the other hand, felt that this special population had a history of poor treatment and discrimination and needed a separate program dedicated to its needs. Signing this MOU, drafted by DOH, without a complete understanding of the past disagreements, complications, and perspectives of DHS staff might have been seen as a rookie mistake, but it also could have led to serious internal problems. DHS staff might have felt unable to trust that the new director had the agency's best interests in mind. Thankfully, my capable secretary was watching my back from the first day.

5 | Getting to Know the Agency and Its Culture; or, Can Anyone Tell Me What's Going On?

No one from the outside can truly understand the day-to-day life and workings of an organization. There is of course the formal organizational chart, which Chandler notes may be a kind of fantasy but also is helpful as a starting point. The chart indicates who has authority—that is, formal power and formal responsibility at each level of the organization. These lines of authority are especially important in public organizations because it is through them that the will of the public, as represented by elected officials, is conveyed. Once inside the organization, a person learns, of course, that not everyone in authority has power and that some people with little formal authority have a great deal of it. Although it contradicts the way things are supposed to work, this is not necessarily a bad thing. The informal life of the organization is commonly the thing that permits people to navigate effectively through a rigid system and get things done.

The organizational chart also shows, though not accurately, who reports to whom. The issue of how many should report to a particular person—or conversely, how many subordinates a director or manager should try to supervise—is an interesting organizational issue. It is referred to as "span of control" in the field of public administration. If the span is too large, the director or manager can't realistically oversee the staff members for whom she or he is responsible. They in turn won't have access to the person to whom they report and from whom they are supposed to get guidance and feedback. There also are serious consequences if the span is too small. In this case, the number of levels in the hierarchy is increased to the point where vertical movement through them slows down everything.

The importance of organizational culture soon became evident to Chandler, as she tells us here. She describes it as a culture of insiders. This is a well-known feature of bureaucracies and certainly is not confined to DHS. (Look, for example, at the federal government's Department of Defense if you want opaqueness. In the private sector, even shareholders have trouble learning about a company in which they are invested). Consumers and scholars have complained about this bureaucratic feature for decades. Sometimes it reflects desires of the agency not to have its inner workings seen by outsiders—such as legislators, *the media, auditors, the general public, and, on occasion, even individuals or offices within the agency itself—and other times, it is simply a reflection of the specialized language of a complex work culture.*

Chandler points out that in her agency, the norm was not to give elected officials any more information than was absolutely required. This is characteristic of the bureaucracy-legislature relationship. To a degree it mimics our relationship as children with our seemingly all-powerful parents to protect our hard-won autonomy. We rationalized, "What they don't know won't hurt them"; but what we really meant was, "What they don't know is less likely to hurt us."

Organizational cultures are important because, by creating shared meanings, they enable people to work together more easily. Assuming that there is going to be such a language, the challenge is how at the same time to promote an organizational climate of transparency. It is also, as Chandler suggests, how to discover ways to communicate more effectively in this complex setting.

The size of DHS's budget really does matter and certainly is an attention getter. In fact, while preparing for the interview with the governor, I read the briefing book and was stunned by the dollar amounts in the budget categories. At one point, I had to stop and count the zeros from right to left until landing at the startling figure of $1.2 billion. After the initial budget shock, the next shock was the fact that there were DHS offices spread out over every island (including Lāna'i) and over two thousand employees. Students in the field of public administration believe that the formal organizational chart is merely a reflection of its author's personal preferences about how she or he would *like* the organization's hierarchy and lines of authority to be. Perhaps organizational charts really are only a rational person's fantasy about how things work, but it seemed to me to be a good starting point, and I wanted to study it. While out of date, the DHS chart did reflect what many people *thought* was the organizational structure. Later, when I worked on a reorganization of some units, the chart was extremely useful as a template. However, it was the DHS telephone directory that became my most helpful and useful tool in discovering who was in the agency and where they worked. Moreover, the directory was a great help in finding the people necessary to talk to and learn from.

Most people don't know the details, size, or structure of a state agency—even those with considerable experience in state government and at the legislature. Even though I had an extensive background in social work and social welfare issues, it became clear that DHS performed a huge number of assigned tasks most people, including me, didn't know about. One month before the start of the job, I had been on sabbatical leave and was enrolled as a student at Syracuse University's Maxwell School of Citizenship and Public Affairs. I was studying for a certificate in public administration by happily writing and extensively researching a paper on organizational theory. Now I was reviewing my class notes and hoping I had acquired the skills necessary to put the great theories into practice at DHS.

The organizational culture at DHS was one of insiders—for insiders. There seemed to be little staff interest in explaining programs and rules to the public, clients, or community advocates—even, at times, to me, the director. This made it difficult for outsiders to find out which DHS office was responsible for what. Even with websites, fliers, posters, mailings, and public service announcements, crucial information was not readily accessible or in a format easily understood. The DHS target group seemed to be the legislature, not the public. The legislators, of course, are the primary funders, and DHS employees knew that they needed information to make budget decisions. Job number one was providing the various legislative committees with just enough information to support the department's budget requests each year. No more and no less.

Written materials produced by the agency were very complex and difficult to decipher unless you had been trained on the inside. We had no public relations person or communications director, and the only printed document was a DHS annual report that after completion went promptly to the state libraries, where it was rarely read. Early on, I issued a directive for the staff to put out department materials for the public only after they passed the director's test. This meant that if the director couldn't understand the materials, even staff-prepared press releases, after reading them once—that is, without needing further explanations or having been previously briefed on the subject—they wouldn't leave the office. As if I were reading student papers at the university, I became the agency's great editor, or grand simplifier. Poor communication may play a major role in the public's low regard for government employees. Better communication, on the other hand, might lead to increased appreciation for what is being accomplished. I think this helped the staff to understand that while they were extremely knowledgeable about DHS policies and procedures, many of our

Department of Human Services Organizational Chart

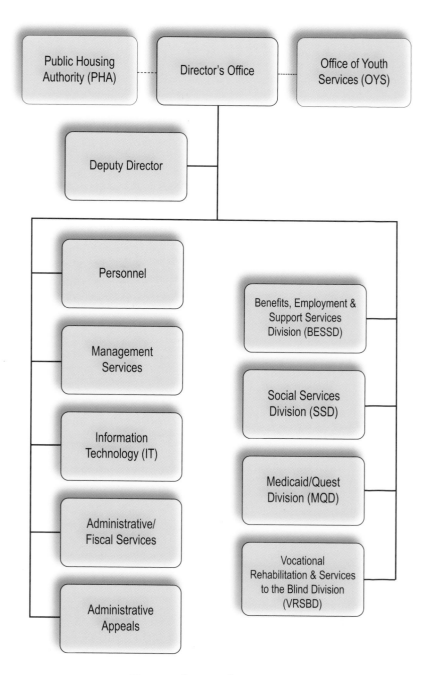

You are where on the org chart?

clients were not—particularly people applying for benefits for the very first time.

The Transition Book; or, What Really Is Going on Here?

This section points to other interesting issues associated with beginning a job as the head of a large public organization. For its successor, each administration is required to provide a transition book, the content of which is up to the departing administrator. The book's purpose is to ease the shift from one administration to another. The one Chandler received was helpful, but left much to be desired in terms of the big-picture changes in social welfare policy, the recent successes and shortfalls of her agency, and the concerns of the previous officeholders. It is easy to imagine the difficult situation of a new director if partisanship were to overcome professionalism in a transition of power from one political party to another.

A reasonable degree of cooperation does not answer the question of what information the transition documents should provide. There are two dimensions to this. The first is how much information. The transition book Chandler describes was large. If such a book is too large, or its sections too detailed, the information won't be used by a new administration, which will soon see discretionary time for reading disappear rapidly. The other issue is the kind of information. It is useful to make a broad distinction between official information—the requirements, rules, and procedural steps that apply to various kinds of budget actions, personnel decisions, and procurement—and the informal type (e.g., Here's what is going on, or How to navigate). This second type would summarize the department's most urgent issues and give tips on how to get things done within or between agencies (e.g., "When you need someone who knows about X, call so-and-so in such and such a department"). Of course, this second kind of information will increase the size of the book and the time needed to prepare it. There is also the possibility that the information provided will lose currency and/or accuracy.

The "Transition Book," mentioned previously, is required by state law to be produced by each department head and is designed to smooth the transition from one administration to the next. Each director includes (or excludes) information as he or she sees fit. This seems like it would be a good document to begin with when starting a new job. Most of the time when one enters a new organization, one reads the mission statement, the goals and objectives, the policy handbook—and promptly falls asleep! This may be when a person asks if she has made a horrible mistake in accepting the job.

The DHS briefing book was over two hundred pages, double spaced, and had no pictures. It was pretty detailed, written in a lot of legalese, and definitely lackluster reading. It was filled with copies of the agency's enabling legislation, administrative rules, policies, federal requirements, and budget documents. Each division administrator had written a section describing his or her role in the bureaucracy. While this was useful in a broad sense, it had an internal orientation (e.g., how papers flow through the organization) and a descriptive tone (i.e., this is how we do things), but very little information about eligibility rules, DHS's clients/customers/consumers and their concerns, and what the agency's budget actually bought (e.g., cost-benefit analysis). There was also no breakdown of services versus administrative costs. The book described how people did their jobs, but seemed to miss the major point that all of these activities should be designed to *serve* clients. It would have been helpful (and important) to know how well that was being done.

Reading the "Transition Book" more carefully a second time generated hundreds of questions. Taking detailed notes produced more questions than notes. I tried to match questions with the staff members who might have the answers—so that I could better understand the agency's inner workings—but this was daunting. While helpful as an overview, the book didn't address the most frequently asked questions, pinpoint the outstanding issues on the DHS plate—such as ongoing lawsuits, new initiatives planned or underway, and anticipated changes—or highlight what the director *really* needed to know about opportunities and challenges. I vowed to write a better one for the next director. I also asked the staff to help me prepare an internal annual report so that we were all aware of the many issues of each year, not just the ones important at transition time. This also helped us create benchmarks for progress and see what we had done well—and still needed to do.

The Early Days; or, Oh Boy...This Is Really Hard!

There is a phenomenon common to many organizations in the public and private sectors: the perpetual crisis. The sense that there is always a crisis that must be dealt with means that, among other things, it is hard to analyze the situation and then take those actions most likely to prevent crises in the first place. This phenomenon may become more prevalent if staff resources are reduced without a significant increase in organizational effectiveness. This sense of perpetual crisis is heightened by a temporal factor. The Hawai'i state legislature meets for only sixty days each year—with recesses, taking from January to May to complete a session—but it occupies a greater proportion of the life of administrative agencies. During the legislative session, everything in a state agency is focused on dealing with legislators. Before the session begins, there is a lot of preparation, and once it ends, there are follow-up and implementation. The legislative session is so important that it makes sense to think of the life of agencies in two phases: the legislative period, and the rest of the year. This compounds the challenges for new directors because their appointments typically coincide with the beginning of the legislative phase, making it even more difficult to understand their organizations and establish meaningful, long-term priorities.

There may be one, but only one area of commonality between Henry Kissinger and me. When he agreed to be the head of the Department of State in President Nixon's administration, he was quoted as saying that he had anticipated the job to be one of discussing significant policy issues and deciding on future directions. The idea that I would be sitting in the director's office and thinking about big policy issues turned out to be pretty naive. Kissinger also incorrectly assumed that the cabinet sat together as the grand thinkers and policy movers of government. In reality, all the easy policy stuff is admirably handled by the staff, and what is left for the appointees are the impossible problems. Any thoughts that the days would be filled with thinking and writing about policy were quickly dashed as it became clear that I had almost no control over my own schedule.

The reality of scheduling is one of moving through problems at an extremely rapid pace, responding to current events, handling crises, and attempting to meet deadlines. There is very little time to plan, muse, or deliberate even though effective-management literature states that doing so is essential for leaders to succeed. From the first day, the department secretary kept the master calendar and booked all of my appointments. Typically the day started at 7:30 a.m. and ended around 7 p.m., and it was usually a six-day week. From January to May, when the state legislature is in session (which turns out to be the longest sixty days imaginable), some part of every day is spent at the legislature or on preparing legislative testimony and/or budgets.

Just a typical day.

The consequence of this is that a person in my position is primarily reacting to events and has little time for working proactively on initiatives, whether organizational or policy focused. The job quickly becomes one of merely managing to keep the boat afloat. In the case of the Cayetano administration, the state's severe budget crisis required each director to absorb significant budget cuts from very early on. This was extremely difficult since most of the newly appointed department directors had not yet had time to figure out what was in the budget, let alone how to design budget-cutting scenarios.

In DHS's case, there are few discretionary funds since most of the welfare program rules, eligibility levels, benefits, and structures are federally designed and mandated. States must follow the rules and regulations exactly in order to receive the federal matching funds that most have become dependent upon. The choices are limited and the degree of flexibility quite constrained, even if a director wants to restrict or cut a program. Most of the programs for the deprived and disabled are protected by state laws and federal mandates precisely so that in difficult economic times states cannot make cuts off the backs of the poor. Programs like Medicaid and food stamps are matched with federal funds. When a legislature cuts funds in an attempt to reduce the state budget, there is a concomitant loss of federal matching funds, which makes such a decision fiscally complex and usually unwise.

The complexities of federal rules and budget requirements are not well understood by legislators, consumers, or the public. The media have an especially hard time understanding agency budget issues or don't want to cover them in depth because they are confusing and not very interesting for most news consumers. During one legislative session, the print media frequently and severely criticized DHS for being fiscally wasteful by making excessive payments to clients. Known as overpayments, they were sent out to clients in the form of cash assistance or food stamps *after* these clients were determined to be ineligible. This amounted to about $2 million a year. Ironically, overpayments occur at DHS even though Hawai'i consistently wins federal bonuses for rating as one of the top three states in the nation for accuracy in food stamp eligibility determination. The payments continued for several reasons: the staff did not get updated information from clients in a timely manner; the information system that received and processed data was rigid, outdated, and slow; and administrative rules designed to protect clients prevented staff from terminating benefits immediately. When a staff member believes a client has become ineligible, the client may appeal the ruling and apply for an administrative hearing.

However, I felt that the most frustrating—and difficult to defend—reason was that the computer systems in place simply were incapable of *stopping* payments in a timely manner. Even when a staff person input a stop-payment order instructing the computer program that a particular person had become ineligible for future benefits—and this required a specific action by an employee, usually a hard-working individual with a caseload of over five hundred clients—that order could not be carried out for several weeks. The computer continued to process payments for at least another benefit cycle, generally fifteen days. Like the *Titanic,* our computer systems could not turn on a dime: they could not stop sending out payments on the day the instruction was entered. In addition, the number of people receiving checks was large (at one time, 160,000 a month) and each family received a variable amount—on average, about $180 a month for food. All these factors multiplied resulted in large overpayments.

Another case of what seems like public sector inefficiency is found in the protection given Hawai'i citizens by DHS's administrative rules. A client may appeal any decision made by a DHS employee that disallows future cash assistance (or any benefit) regardless of the reason. Until the dispute is resolved, assistance will continue. An administrative hearing must be held within ninety days. A decision to terminate a benefit may be made only after that hearing is held and a formal disposition is made. Even when the client loses the case and is deemed ineligible for the benefit, the benefit has to be continued until the appeal process is completed. And while it is extremely rare for a client to prevail, since staff determinations are usually correct, it is also extremely difficult to get money back from a financially strapped person who is no longer receiving cash assistance. Thus the amount of money paid to ineligible clients grows each year, and the press of course shouts about departmental overpayments.

One sunny morning, the front page of a daily newspaper headlined that DHS overpayments had reached $40 million. This number astounded both DHS and the governor. I immediately went into crisis mode, and it took me hours just to understand the legal definition of an overpayment, why DHS had so many, and how the intricacies of the computer and mailing systems had contributed to the problem. The most amazing thing I learned was that the Department of the Attorney General (DoAG) actually had control of the DHS overpayment system: these payments were considered bad debts—ones that the state agency was confident would never be paid back. Even dead people's names could not be removed from the list of bad debts without the attorney general's investigation and approval. This usually took *years*. (DoAG is also understaffed, and its attorneys did not see this as a very high priority.) So, on paper, millions of dollars seemed to have been given away to undeserving people, and DHS was blamed even though another state department was tasked with closing out the finding. This seemed extraordinarily wasteful and was an easy target for media reporters investigating inefficiency and ineffective government. The newspaper only told the story of the excesses—not the constraints, the complications, or the additional staffing required. And even when the department tried to hire, on a contingency basis, a private collection agency to help collect past-due money, none would take the job since it was so unlikely that any money would be returned.

6

If Only the Boss Really Had Power; or, It's Not So Lonely at the Top

One of the reasons we want to move up the organizational ladder is that we can finally be in a position to decide important issues. No more having to do what the boss says or looking for opportunities to smuggle in a thought. Even if we are aware that we don't always do what our boss says, we think that if we get to the pinnacle of the organization, then we will be in a position to do good work. That is, of course, true and, disconcertingly, not true. CEOs do have more positional authority, and that is a source of power. Real power must be gathered from diverse sources and can be difficult to exercise. Under the best of circumstances, it must be marshaled and wielded carefully. Systems, private as well as public, constrain all of us, even those at the top. In this section Chandler provides a glimpse into the odd experience of feeling trapped inside a seemingly powerful position.

Being the chief executive officer of a large state agency seems like it would enable you to have a lot of power, and in some ways it does. But in many other ways, you really are simply riding a horse in the direction it wants to go. Most staff employees of public agencies do jump when asked to complete tasks. However, it is often necessary for the boss to say, "This is a mandate," in order to ensure compliance. "This is an order" is a phrase not used a lot by social workers or professors. Though using it is not considered acceptable management style, at times it was required. Sometimes, supervisors would play the "director said" game. This was a strategy in which they would tell their subordinates that the director said they should do this or not do that. Frequently, the only way I learned this was by being at a meeting where I heard that a unit was doing something (or not) because "the director said so." Often I had never even heard about the issue.

Organizationally, the director's office *seemed* powerful since all outgoing ideas about legislation, budget requests, position redescriptions, contracts, and so forth needed my authorization. However, the director must rely on the advice of her staff since it would be impossible to conduct business if the director and deputy director were required to review every decision being made. The agency would come to a screeching halt. Exceptions included the legislative agenda and budget, which were top priorities: every piece of legislation and every budget request were carefully and painstakingly reviewed in the director's office.

There is power in not signing a bill or budget request. Even asking for more information, justification, and explanation is power. However, as discussed in the next section, procuring and contracting for services is a complex process in which other state agencies, such as DoAG, human resources, B&F, and accounting and general services all exert heavy influence over DHS and its director. Power is shared across many state agencies and also with the governor and the legislature. These agencies function as staff agencies to those like DHS and DOH, and often their directors' signatures are required for hiring, budget changes, leases, contracts…all from the petty to the sublime.

7

Finding the Right Help; or, with a Little Help from My Friends

Chandler's job was made easier and she made more successful because she was able to hire an excellent private secretary. That tells us how important support positions are. It also tells us that, in this sense, she may have gotten lucky. Secretarial positions were exempt (not civil service), so technically they were open to anyone, regardless of previous employment, experience, or qualifications. (Coming from the university, she had no secretary of her own to bring along.) She was introduced to only two potential candidates. Both had experience in the department and were supported by the previous director and deputy director. They were presented to her as loyal people requesting placement in the new administration. Hiring from the outside would have added to the challenges posed by Chandler's inexperience.

Chandler searched for and recognized different skills in her staff. The idea people were valuable in helping her think through sticky problems and devise solutions. However, these people tended not to be the same ones who were the most effective in getting the day-to-day work done. The idea people were more creative and were risk takers; other staff members were more conservative and risk adverse. This difference raises an interesting question about what kind of employee we want in our public agencies. Should we select the innovators and adventurers or those who focus on consistency and detail? The adventurers will appeal to reformers looking for more flexible, responsive organizations; the steady implementers will appeal to staff concerned about the public's need for predictability and accountability. Each type will produce a different kind of organizational culture. In the end, as Chandler points out, we must balance our desire for public organizations that are flexible and adaptive with our need for organizations that are consistent and equitable.

The challenge of putting together a team is accentuated by constraints on hiring new employees. Exempt positions may be filled outside of the civil service system. These positions do not have minimum qualifications, experience requirements, seniority protections, or the benefits and protections of civil service jobs. Under the rules in place at that time, employees within the department who met a position's minimum qualifications, as set by the personnel office, had first option for an in-house job.

Why is there such a rule? These bureaucracies are what is referred to as merit based: people who serve in them are highly qualified for this work because the hiring, retention, and promotion system is based on merit. The merit-based system replaced the patronage system in the late nineteenth century as a way to create a professional and impartial public bureaucracy. It is also a way of creating incentives for people to remain in positions that often pay less than their counterparts in the private sector, and preserves stability and experience in a public agency when elections cause changes in leadership.

Describing these systems as merit based is of course questionable. Public bureaucracies have succeeded in providing protection from dismissal for partisan reasons and have made it more difficult (though far from impossible) for elected officials to burrow their loyal followers into the system. Moreover, hiring procedures must objectively differentiate the applicants. Nevertheless, over time public sector bureaucracies have come to be more seniority oriented than merit based. Almost without regard to the quality of a person's work, seat time plays a major role in promotions and makes it difficult to get the best people into available positions. This has the effect of giving employees a predictable career ladder and assuring them a high degree of job security, but it also means they are supervised by managers who may have gotten into their positions for the wrong reasons, making it more difficult for them to effectively fulfill their responsibilities.

Given this history, and the expectation there would be a pool of qualified persons to select from, the situation raises the following questions. Would the work of public employees, and the public orientation of their organizations, be enhanced if the recruitment process was open to competition from public, private, and nonprofit sector applicants? Would better persons be found to do the job? Or would this change undermine public service professionalism, and perhaps even introduce a new form of patronage?

There is a need for two types of employees in public sector agencies: people who have not worked in government, who see the issues differently, and who can bring fresh ideas and creativity to public sector problems; and people who are willing and able to operate within the constraints of a bureaucracy, who follow rules easily, and who can tolerate incremental improvements over a long period. Since employees in public sector agencies are mostly civil servants or contractors from the private sector, directors rarely have the opportunity to put together a fresh administrative team. They must depend on the staff members already there. And because of the fiscal shortfall, the Cayetano administration was forced to establish a hiring freeze. I had no opportunity to fill new administrative positions or form my own administrative team. Even external consultants were few and far between. It is extremely difficult in Hawai'i's public sector, even under the best of circumstances, to hire outside the civil service system and put together a team made up of new employees. Civil service rules and regulations are quite constraining, and staff in the state's personnel office usually interpret the rules narrowly. They too are understaffed, so decisions often take many months. Changing the civil service laws (which takes legislative action) or changing a civil service position to an exempt position (one without protections and seniority) is required to ease these hiring regulations.

Hiring non–civil service employees to do the work of government is rare in Hawai'i. Perhaps it is a legacy of the history of strong unions both in the public and private sectors. The Hawai'i Government Employees Association, the United Public Workers (UPW), and the Hawai'i State Teachers' Association are powerful voices at the state legislature and have negotiated many employee protections. Many see both civil service protections and the public sector unions as obstacles to what modern

We evaluate talent closely.

public managers need: flexibility in employee hiring and firing; and the overall ability to be responsive in a rapidly changing environment. In response to some of these complaints, the legislature changed the law to permit managed competition—allowing public employees to compete with private sector companies for new contracts—but the provisions were cumbersome and rarely used. Finding the balance that provides adequate wages and appropriate working conditions—as well as permits public sector agencies to be flexible enough to meet changing needs—remains a challenge.

I had heard many horror stories and complaints about the public sector unions in Hawai'i. Most people outside of government blame the unions for almost every inefficiency that has ever existed in a public agency. If things are bad, it is *because of the unions*. As the daughter of a union attorney, and someone who had worked for a union in New York City, I began with a positive view of the role that unions play in protecting the rights of workers. Early on, I thought it would be a good idea to meet some of the union stewards

The state civil service policy called Internal Vacancy Announcement (IVA) requires that all announcements for new hiring be advertised first inside the agency, then inside all the other state agencies. Then, and only then, may outside candidates apply. Persons within the agency often would be deemed qualified and considered eligible by the personnel office based on their experience within the agency. The result is that it is difficult for a manager to recruit a person from outside the agency because an internal candidate is defined as qualified for the job by meeting the minimum qualifications and has preference over anyone else. However, the job requirements themselves may have changed (or need to be changed), and a person with different attributes and skills may now be needed. Most states do not have such strict hiring and seniority requirements. Simultaneous advertising and broadbanding position descriptions permit more hiring flexibility. New directors in most states are able to select and bring in a few new members of their team to assist in moving a new agenda along. This is very difficult in Hawai'i.

at DHS in an effort to hear complaints and learn about issues. I also wanted to introduce myself as a person who was a trained mediator and believed that there were many problem-solving and alternative dispute-resolving strategies available that could be used before formal labor-management grievances were filed and lawsuits or arbitration became necessary. So I invited one shop steward to lunch. "No deal." Each one I asked told me that he could not go anywhere with me and could not even be seen with me unless we were negotiating a settlement. Each explained that even seeing me informally to discuss the types of concerns union members were sharing might look like collusion. It seemed to me that this was not an enlightened labor-management system. So much for early problem solving!

In this context, my task was to search among the staff for the stars. It was essential to quickly find people who could explain things clearly and accurately. They might not necessarily be the people highlighted on the organizational chart: supervisors, branch chiefs, section administrators, and division administrators. Locating the brains and talent sometimes seemed like a treasure hunt. There were clues, but they could be a bit obscure. I had to identify people who were open to change, who shared my perspective, and who had the skills and knowledge to explain how the place really worked.

Assessing the talent within an organization is difficult because individual strengths might not be apparent. Employees come with multiple and highly variable skills. Early on, I leaned toward those who seemed to be the most interesting people—the ones who liked to discuss policy ideas and options about welfare reform, budget scenarios, and new approaches to contracting for services. Often, however, the people with the most interesting ideas were not the most knowledgeable about how to get things done. Their advice was sometimes based on their own failures to make needed changes or on their personal frustrations. The people who knew how the place really worked—and could make the trains run on time—seemed quite conservative. As essential as they were, I didn't reach out to them at first, but later learned I had to.

8 | Speaking in Different Tongues; or, When Cultures Meet

There are at least two reasons to consult with staff and involve them in deliberations about what should or should not be done. The first is that we gain from their knowledge and insight. The individuals who actually deliver the programs on a daily basis understand what is and isn't working, and often know what might be done to improve things. The other reason is that their being included and allowed to participate will make them more likely to accept what is decided, even if it isn't what they would have chosen.

The issue Chandler is pointing to is how to get staff engaged. Her experience is that (1) most staff don't see such deliberations as part of their real work, (2) they are too ready to defer to authority figures in the hierarchy, and (3) they sometimes withhold information as a way of protecting the director. The challenge, then, is how to create a higher volume of what we might refer to as critical talk: that is, exchanges in which people feel it is acceptable, or even obligatory, to share their knowledge and ideas.

At least three things may be necessary. First, leaders must consistently provide a safe and rewarding environment for opinions to be expressed. Next, staff members need to be given some training in problem solving, group deliberation, and communicating their ideas so that others will hear them. Finally, there has to be transition time: it is not reasonable to expect that individuals who have not been asked their opinions, or who have been spanked for giving them, will suddenly transform themselves into open and engaged staff members.

Chandler observes that information sharing was a daily Herculean task and provides a nice example of why. It is interesting to speculate on the degree to which new information technology systems can solve these problems. Will they improve the information-sharing functions, or will we find that the technology simply comes to reflect the shortcomings of the organizational systems that produced it?

The challenge of understanding how things worked around DHS was not helped by my ingrained professorial style of asking questions, thinking out loud, brainstorming, making suggestions, probing, and playing with policy options before making a decision. The questioning and challenging style common among the faculty at a university could be quite upsetting to staff used to attending meetings in which the director was mostly informing everyone about a particular course of action she had already decided on.

The culture of the organization had been to have each division administrator or staff officer meet alone with the director, either to learn what had been decided or to ask how to implement directives. The staff, therefore, found it extremely uncomfortable to be asked questions by the director or to be encouraged to freely offer opinions. Often, staff took the director's ideas and musings as decisions rather than efforts to try to figure things out.

Since the staff seemed quite uncomfortable with deliberative dialogues and discussion sessions, a system was designed by the deputy director. She explained that the director would raise her hand in the air—perhaps like a student in class—to signal that she was just trying out an idea or thinking about something and was not anywhere near making a decision. This took some training. Once, a staff person asked if we were done thinking so everyone could get back to work. Frequently, staff asked if the director was mandating a particular action and, if so, it would be obeyed. Otherwise, some people wondered, what were they doing at the meeting? The deputy director often had the job of explainer or translator, and a few times she needed to stop rumors that were running rampant in the department because I had shared a brainstorming idea or a thought with someone.

The university and many private sector organizations thrive on dialogue and sharing information and new ideas. While there was rich expertise inside the DHS bureaucracy, it was often narrowly defined and specialized. Many employees believed they should stick to their knitting, meaning their assigned jobs as they understood them. It may be more common for a director to assemble a small team to think about options and then bring in people who will need to implement decisions. I believed that bringing staff from many levels to the table for initial discussions, while unusual, strengthened the final product. I felt that explaining this approach more clearly and practicing the approach more regularly would have helped the employees understand how their participation was valued and genuinely sought. It also would have helped me understand their reluctance to participate.

Many staff members saw their goal as protecting the new director from looking bad, which was defined as making a mistake in public. Unfortunately, this manifested itself in a variety of negative ways. At times, information was withheld and bad news wasn't shared. For example, information about being sued, or a federal rule change, was often hard to obtain. Instead, the person responsible for a particular area would arrange a meeting to break the news. However, she rarely came with the relevant paperwork or documentation to study or review. The modus operandi seemed to be to share as little information as possible for as long as possible, rather than provide too much information too soon. This could be seen either as maintaining their power or protecting the new appointee from saying something that could have negative consequences later. Some staff members assumed that a director would not speak if he or she didn't know much—a risky assumption.

The media were often purveyors of bad news. I often would not hear of something that had happened somewhere in the department until the press asked me for a comment. I got to expect this when a legislative audit report was about to hit the front page. Over time I got better at predicting when the press would call. Sometimes we would be asked to comment on something that the governor had said in a press conference but that we were unaware of. This is how we learned that one of our divisions, PHA, was moving from DHS to DBEDT.

Face to Face with Staff; or, How Do You Find Out What Is Really Going On?

Hierarchies, both private and public, make it hard for people to speak outside their roles and say what needs to be said. Individuals of lower rank may feel it is not their place to speak. No one wants to fail, look stupid, or be seen as betraying his or her colleagues. Information is also a source of power, and a director proposing that more be shared may threaten people who control either the information or the channel.

While there are no foolproof solutions, some things can help. Chandler's personal style, which is less formal, projects interest, invites interactions, makes her appear approachable, and provides the right role model. It may not work for everyone, but it will be more effective than appearing distant or aloof and insisting on being addressed by the proper title.

A clearly signaled willingness to listen can also help. Sometimes it is possible for the director to establish the practice of simply walking around to offices or of being available in high-traffic areas like break rooms or near water coolers (although in an agency as large and spread out as DHS this was not a good option). Of course, as Chandler makes clear by the approach she took, consistency of effort in finding ways to learn what is on people's mind also is critical.

Suggestion boxes are one such way. A contemporary version of this is an email address dedicated to employee opinions, feedback, and ideas for improvement. If morale is not good, however, this can generate a seemingly endless stream of personal complaints about things that ultimately don't matter much. When trust is low, employees are more reluctant to identify themselves, and if comments are anonymous, responding to them constructively may be awkward. As Chandler points out, the presence of a chain of command does not encourage employees to openly share their ideas.

Doing a walkabout around the agency seemed like a terrific way to learn what was going on in DHS. Physically visiting the hundreds of small units and offices to hear directly from staff was a strategy to open lines of communication. The deputy director and I hoped to visit every unit across the state. The administrative assistant, who had worked for the agency for several years, offered to introduce us. When we were introduced to the first unit as the "Dir" (short for "Director") and the "D-Dir" (short for "Deputy Director"), we burst out laughing because to us it sounded like "dumb" and "dumber"! No one else thought it funny, but with each introduction, we had to contain our giggles. Finally we asked to be introduced by our names.

After taking an entire morning to walk through the major administrative offices in our building, we were asked if we wanted to do this for all the remaining offices. We estimated this would take about six weeks of solid traveling across Oʻahu and the neighbor islands. Since the legislature was then in session, this would be impossible. We did, however, set up a schedule to ensure that we would physically visit every office in the state. Some visits were not made till many months into my first term.

Maybe a hammer would work?

We started an annual Xmas-in-July Visit. We brought a small gift or food (paid for out of our personal funds) to thank the staff for its hard work.

Sometimes the visits were in July, and sometimes we didn't get there until December. The walkabouts provided us with an in-depth view of what was going on from both the clients' and employees' perspectives. What we learned was very helpful in understanding the needs of the organization as well as the community.

Some staff, usually the supervisors, didn't like these visits and expressed fear someone might complain. The personnel office advised me *Law and Order* style that anything I said could be used against me in a court of law (or more likely at an arbitration or grievance hearing). Later, I would ask a staff person why this or that hadn't been fixed or followed up on after the visits. The stock response was, "Which unit were you visiting?" or "Who told you that?" Often there was a defensive quality to these responses. Despite this, I believed strongly in conducting these visits and saw them as a way to learn about the agency from employees at all levels.

After the first round of visits, it became clear to me that staff opportunities to meet with previous directors had been pretty rare. My sessions usually began with me talking about new legislative initiatives, budget cuts, or program initiatives. I assumed these were topics of interest to the staff. I learned quickly that staff preoccupations were much more internal than external. Questions ranged from "Why did you take away the automatic postal meter?" to "Are you in favor of reducing the hours that the welfare offices remain open to the public?" Often the questions were quite specific: personnel matters, travel policies, complaints about supervisors. At first I would try to move the conversation back to my important issues, which I thought should be theirs. However, they were concerned about their workspace, their colleagues, their paperwork, too many clients, et cetera—not what was taking place in the director's office. This was the real stuff of work life in the bureaucracy.

I took very detailed notes at these visits and promised to get back to employees with answers. I gathered information about their concerns but was repeatedly told to turn problems over to their supervisor or administrator. This rarely did the trick. These types of problems took too long to solve if dropped back into the bureaucracy and slipped under all of the other issues that required attention. We developed a feedback system with a specific timeline so that promises to the staff could be fulfilled. Sometimes we heard a terrific idea or suggestion that seemed reasonable to implement. Unfortunately, the response might be an extraordinarily complicated memo documenting why the idea or suggestion couldn't be implemented. It took staff a long time to research and prepare these responses, which irritated them and usually didn't meet the needs of the affected employees. Although I tried to honor their confidentiality, sometimes it backfired, with the employee who had made the suggestion being asked to do the extra work of writing the response.

A suggestion box was placed in each office, and any employee could directly call or email the director. Few ever did. Fear of losing a job and fear of retaliation were strong. Honoring the chain of command was seen as essential for good organizational operations. Violating it was seen as disrespectful to the upper levels. Trying to get information to improve operations was also seen as disrespectful. I sometimes worried that the command-and-control style of communication among the staff would be replicated with the clients. It was clear to me that organizational reforms were necessary within DHS if improvements in meeting our clients' needs were going to take place.

Shortly after I started, I saw a memo that had been drafted with a note asking for my signature. It was a condolence note. Four people had signed off on the letter prior to it reaching my desk. I asked the personnel officer to explain why so many reviews were needed to send out this letter. This was an early attempt to try to streamline the levels and lines of communication in the hierarchy. It was also an early failure.

The answer I received was that the person who had the death in the family is eligible for funeral leave. The policy requires that the employee's supervisor needs to inform the section administrator who informs the division administrator who informs the personnel office so the leave form can be processed correctly. The initials on the side of the letter verify that each level has been notified appropriately. I guess the fear is that

- *a person who is absent from work would not have had his or her leave papers filled out accurately (sick leave, vacation leave, funeral leave), and*

- *a person would mistakenly receive a condolence note.*

Reducing the number of signatures appeared to be non-negotiable. However, there was one little success. I changed the signature line on the condolence note to remove all of my professional initials. At least that much could be altered to make the note somewhat more personal.

9 | The DHS Storybook; or, Hunting and Gathering

What is it that the heads of large public departments must know, and what shouldn't they have to know? Or, as Chandler points out, from the staff's point of view what are they better off not knowing?

Under Chandler, DHS took an interesting approach to meeting divergent information requirements: it created the "DHS Storybook." The "Storybook" began as a compilation of facts, but gradually evolved into something useful for planning—and perhaps for transitions between administrations. It pushed DHS in the direction of establishing goals, benchmarks, and outcomes. Its creation also is a nice example of being inventive in changing the practices of large, conservative agencies.

These kinds of tools have become popular as replacements for the way agencies traditionally saw their work, which was in terms of how many clients they saw, how many contracts they wrote, how many cases they handled—that is, their output. These tools also are more demanding. Outcomes, for example, ask the agency to demonstrate that what it does makes a difference in terms of its most basic purposes. These normally are much harder, and more time consuming, to measure, or even define, than goals or output. Measuring outcomes requires a substantial investment in training, as well as a change in attitude about what constitutes success.

Because there needed to be a single source for information about DHS and relevant information was hard to find, we created the "DHS Storybook." (This was something quite different from the annual report or "Transition Book" described earlier.)

For example, whenever a director goes to a legislative hearing, there is an expectation that he or she will know the answers to just about every question asked, whether by a legislator, consumer, or advocacy group. Some legislators expect the director to answer questions, no matter how detailed, and are miffed when the director asks his or her administrator for help or even looks at an agency sourcebook.

Usually, my staff had not thought about these issues in political terms and therefore didn't see the necessity of preparing for basic questions about programs or services. Most were experts on budgets and legislation, but few had the public relations skills often needed at the legislature. They felt that if the legislators had not asked those questions before, there was no need to prepare for such a contingency. Isn't it better to wait until asked and then say you will respond later? For example, one health insurance plan believed that it had a larger percentage of high-risk pregnancies among its enrollees and thus was spending more on its patients than the other plans. It therefore wanted more money as a risk-adjustment supplement. Another plan contended that it had more patients with

This is getting curiouser and curiouser.

HIV/AIDS, and still another worried that it had more Native Hawaiians in its plan who were at high risk of getting certain costly diseases, such as diabetes. These data were not routinely collected since the Medicaid program in Hawai'i was a managed-care program using a per person–per month reimbursement system to the health plans. Questions about how many people were in each plan were considered important to the staff since the budget was based on this. However, questions like how many people had specific health problems were not.

I saw the need for a new type of agency publication. The "DHS Storybook" described all of the services and programs of the agency; what was funded by state dollars, and what funded by federal dollars; the clients being served (i.e., demographics); and what the agency was predicting as its future needs. The "Storybook" became crucial to managing the department and providing information to the community. It was essential to legislators in their efforts to understand and support DHS while they also attempted to balance the budget in fiscally challenging times.

Over the years, the "Storybook" moved from describing things to establishing goals, benchmarks, and outcomes. However, trying to move from what the department always had done to an outcome-accountability focus was very hard work. Measurement issues are challenging in public sector

> *The first storybook was a strange product. To make it more readable, I suggested that we add pictures in the various sections and make it look more like a "Storybook" that would tell the story of DHS. Confidentiality rules prohibit the use of clients' photos without their express written permission, so I suggested that we use pictures of the staff and their children, parents, grandparents, and so forth to begin each section. Not a single staff member volunteered family pictures. I subsequently learned that many of the employees thought it would be dreadful to be in the DHS Storybook since someone might think they or their family members were DHS recipients! Undaunted, I collected old baby photos of my child and my in-laws as needy seniors. My own mother became the "DHS Storybook" cover girl. I wondered if this episode meant that staff morale was so low that even they saw the services they provided as stigmatizing.*

work. Was the agency successful in preventing child abuse? Did the drug treatment programs prevent future relapses? Was the investment in early childhood education sufficient? By the state's providing more health insurance to children under Medicaid, would these children be healthier adults? Was working part-time in a minimum-wage job really putting someone on the road to self-sufficiency? Was providing a cash incentive to a single mom to marry the father of her baby good public policy? How could we measure these results? Which was the responsibility of the agency and which the responsibility of the public? Who was really responsible for these outcomes? Were we able to design measures to adequately and appropriately capture the information necessary for program review and evaluation?

Changing from doing the job as it had always been done (the work process) to measuring effectiveness was a big leap. Part of the problem was that DHS and other public sector agencies had neither clearly defined objectives to which they could be held accountable nor information systems to gather the data necessary to accurately measure outcomes. In addition, the employees didn't have a clear sense of how their roles and responsibilities fit into the department's agenda.

The "DHS Storybook" became a progress report that not only better documented the activities and services we were providing, but also the staff's growing understanding of how to measure outcomes. The first year, I wrote the "Storybook" myself. I requested chapters from the division administrators and developed a template for each to submit materials. However, since clear measurable objectives had not been agreed to previously, publishing the "Storybook" each year became a way to describe new activities, to document success, and to explain to the public and the legislators what DHS was doing. Some other departments followed suit, and eventually the governor's office tried to use the "Storybook" as a model for the administration's achievements.

I think this was a mini-success story primarily because it helped boost employee morale: the department could clearly see the progress it was making. It helped externally also: many legislators, particularly the new ones, asked for a copy so they could get a better understanding of DHS's programs and services.

10 | Meeting the Legislature; or, Honoring the Honorables

The Hawai'i legislative session is only about four months long, but it still has a huge impact on the work rhythms and loads of executive agencies. For many agencies, it can seem like everything else is put on hold during the mobilization prior to and during the session. This is even more the case if hot-button issues bring legislators to the agency's doorstep.

During the rest of the year, a sensible answer to the question of what the director should know might be that she or he needs to know enough to make sound leadership decisions, provide support, and communicate with the agency's various stakeholders. As we saw in the previous section, the response during session, quite different, is that the director must know whatever a legislator thinks she or he should. This points to the complicated relationship between department heads and legislators. Because they belong to different branches of government and are trying to fulfill different kinds of public responsibilities, their relationships can be difficult, even volatile, as is sometimes seen in public hearings. Chandler notes the importance of the director understanding this political dynamic.

Much of this section focuses on the interesting issue of where legislators obtain their information. This has special importance because legislators inevitably will be uninformed about many of the myriad issues they have to vote on. Chandler comments on three different information sources—resources within the legislative branch, public hearings, and administrative departments—while mentioning several others. Each has advantages and limitations. For reasons that have little to do with the personalities of the individuals involved, the most complex source is the administrative department.

It should be remembered that this description does not include those whose job is to provide specific information to legislators; that is, lobbyists. If Chandler had been director of a department that more directly affected the interests of large businesses, lobbyists would have been more a part of the process.

A major difference between public and private organizations is the huge role that the state legislature plays in the life of the public ones. All policies affecting an agency must be passed by the legislature. Every budget item, program change, and employee position number must be approved by the legislature. Every question asked by a legislator should be responded to promptly, no matter how farfetched or difficult to answer. For example, an agency may be asked to predict the number of children who are likely to be abused or neglected next year. If the number provided is underestimated, legislators criticize the agency for not knowing its clientele. If the number is overestimated, the agency is criticized for trying to hoard money that could have been spent elsewhere.

In Hawai'i, legislation is often written with extensive detail, designed to provide very little wiggle room for agencies and to constrain their actions. Some legislators get overly involved in the details and daily workings of agencies. Others function more like board members of a nonprofit agency and remain at the policy level. Which legislator is selected chairperson of the subject committee thus affects an agency immensely.

While it is the taxpayers who are ultimately the bosses of all public agencies and the legislators who are the policy directors, the community is often unfamiliar with this relationship. In public administration terms, there is a tug-of-war between efficiency and responsiveness. If an agency needed only to get welfare checks out on time, it could be done quite efficiently. However, the public sector staff must ensure that the recipients are eligible, talk to them, answer questions, answer phones, and be monitored by auditors at the federal, state, and local levels. In addition, staff members must respond to a huge variety of questions from the director, the media, advocates, and legislators.

While it *is* the responsibility of the agency to provide as much information as possible, multiple hearings on different topics—Medicaid, child welfare, food stamps, job training, childcare, blind vendors, et cetera—require a significant amount of preparation time. The director must take along the division administrators to answer very specific policy or procedural questions, but they too are working on many other tasks and priorities. Clients often show up at these hearings with terrible stories that have a big impact and make a big media splash. Oftentimes, after the agency has researched the issue and complete information has been provided, the facts appear quite different. By then, however, legislators have moved on to other issues. Holding public hearings may not be the most efficient or effective way to discuss policy reform.

Public hearings on changes to the federally mandated requirements of the state's welfare program provide interesting examples. Every state was required to limit welfare benefits to a maximum of five years and also require work, job searches, or training to all able-bodied clients. Many people disliked these requirements, and frequently a client would go to a legislative hearing and testify about someone he or she knew who either wasn't getting the benefits deserved or was being required to do something that someone else wasn't. The department could only discuss policies and procedures—not individual circumstances—even if it knew about the particular case, which it usually didn't. Testifiers often spoke eloquently about their own problems or those of family members whom they believed were being treated unfairly. At times, the legislators would want to investigate these stories and even suggest policy changes to prevent such incidents from happening again. The problem from the department's perspective was that it rarely had the information it needed to follow up on the case (e.g., name, address, or phone number) and sometimes the description of the situation was not completely

For example, questions like the following are common. "How many Hawaiians are on welfare?" "How many on Medicaid?" "What! You don't collect data on ethnicity from the Medicaid clients? Why not?" "Isn't it true that Hawaiians have higher health-care costs?" "Shouldn't you have special programs for them?" "Why don't you expand Medicaid to all low-income children?" "Oh, the legislature needs to fund that by putting more money into the agency's budget? How much more? Why don't they do that? Did you ask them?" Each of these questions would require data and policy research to appropriately answer.

Staff spends a lot of time responding to these inquiries. There are few public information officers left in public agencies these days, so such questions are referred to staff members, who are already busy with client and agency tasks. Acquiring new information or doing data runs costs money, but none is budgeted. Moreover, the questions are being asked of offices that are already short staffed and underfunded to maintain basic agency operations or client services. (This is even truer today than when I was the director.) This frustrates the consumers, the public, legislators, and DHS.

accurate. Stories about people losing their health insurance were extremely disturbing. Federal Medicaid eligibility rules are extremely complex and arcane, and though it would seem as if the Medicaid office were preventing people from obtaining health insurance, its goal was to get people insured.

Perhaps the most emotional and distressing stories were reports about child protection cases in which people would complain that DHS swept in and took a child away from a family when it shouldn't have or that the department didn't remove a child when it should have. Of course, I wanted all the information I could get about problems in our service-delivery system and would follow up on any complaint about a worker being rude or a service being poorly delivered. However, it is difficult to problem solve in a public setting without the complete facts.

Steven Tepper (2004) discusses the role of strategic forums in constructing policy dialogues that help clarify agendas among different interest groups and/or may help policymakers better understand available options and the tradeoffs of each action. Policy dialogues or public deliberation strategies are more commonly used to craft policy strategies and set directions. These community-based approaches, often using the skills of a trained facilitator, may be more effective than a public hearing to get information shared and ideas about important policy options discussed.

Since legislators are the policymakers and oversee the programs and budgets of the public agencies, they need to become knowledgeable about those budgets. The chairs of subject committees like human services, education, and health, after listening to the agencies and the advocates, often become supporters and take the budget requests to the finance committees (the House Finance Committee or the Senate Ways and Means Committee). Fully informing them is essential for the funding of the agency.

In Hawai'i, individual legislators have little capacity to conduct their own research on policy matters, bills, or legislation. The Legislative Reference Bureau and the Legislative Auditor's Office do not have sufficient staff or expertise to provide legislators with quick responses to questions and with budget predictions or forecasts. Neither do they have the ability to provide legislators with comparative information from other states about policy initiatives.

The political party offices provide some information across states, but the most useful organizations are the National Governors Association and the National Council of State Legislatures. However, these resources often provide dated program-level, and descriptive write-ups and are not terribly helpful to legislators in the midst of a session. Ultimately, legislators must depend on state agency staff for answers. They often don't trust these data and they rarely like the answers provided, but they keep asking.

What often happens, whether intentionally or not, is that the agencies cannot (or do not) provide the data quickly or in a comprehensible format for the legislators, especially if the bill being considered is not seen as directly beneficial to the agency. Often, the department's mantra when requested to provide information is, "Yes, I will send you the information you requested at a later time." Later may become never, and darn! The session is over. DHS often had many of the stock answers in the "Storybook" and presented them to legislators multiple times throughout the session. This helped a bit.

Because the legislators don't have other sources of information, they may ask the departments to help them with the passage of a bill despite a department's wariness. If the bill requires funding in addition to the governor's budget request or is a statutory change that was not in the governor's administrative package, the agency should not publicly support the bill. This is because the agency is in the executive branch, not the legislative branch, and any new bill will be outside the governor's initial legislative package and beyond the agency's (and the governor's) budget request. Legislators may get quite miffed when the executive branch does not support their ideas. Often, agencies are asked to cost out a legislator's proposal or analyze a particular bill. Many times what comes back from the agency are details of the true costs of the new proposal—a response often seen as obstructionist.

Relationships matter, and the agency administrator must keep his or her legislative committee members well informed and must continue responding to all requests and proposals. This can be very tricky and time consuming. Departments often develop good working relationships with nonprofits that can become a buffer between them and unhappy legislators. Nonprofits are an excellent source of information about community needs but also are strong advocates of the agencies doing more and contracting for more services.

Sometimes legislators want to require a department's staff to do a particular thing for him or her. When this goes beyond a legislator's policy role and moves into administration, the agency simply can't comply. For example, after a particularly horrible child abuse case, legislative hearings were held to ensure that the situation never occurred again. In this news-making case, there was a breakdown in communication among the police department, a hospital, and the Child Protective Services (CPS) branch of DHS. Legislators wanted to pass a piece of legislation requiring hospitals to check with the police and CPS whenever they suspected abuse or neglect to see if the child had ever been in the CPS system. This information was impossible to share due to federal and state privacy laws. These hearings produced a great deal of anger on the part of the citizens (and the press) attending, recriminations among the different agencies involved, and what appeared to be a lack of concern or appreciation of the tragic event among the public agencies.

Legislative Oversight; or, "Say What?"

Here is a look at another aspect of the relations between the legislature and administrative agencies. Since legislators are the representatives of the public, doesn't it make sense that they determine, to the greatest degree possible, the content of the bills they pass? That is, why don't legislators always tell the agencies, through the language of the bill, exactly what they want done? When they don't, much of what actually happens is left up to the agency's administrative staff members, who are not elected.

There are at least three reasons legislation is not more specific than it could be. One is that there simply is too little time to work out all of the necessary details. The second, related to the first, is that in most cases legislators do not have the detailed knowledge required to write these bills well. As Chandler points out, when highly prescriptive legislation is formulated badly, it creates significant problems. Finally, and perhaps most important, legislators very often cannot agree on important elements of a bill, not to mention its details. Given this disagreement, they craft legislation that is general enough to garner support for passage without raising divisive issues. This frequently means a bill's provisions are quite broad.

The administrative staff members, by the act of giving specificity to bills, also become policymakers. Recognizing this, Americans have attempted to control the policymaking power by creating a complex system of administrative rule making. Each time an agency, in making the decisions necessary to implement a piece of legislation, creates a rule that affects the public, it must conduct an administrative hearing. This process offers the public an opportunity to participate in the rule making. Of course, these rules, however made, are the same ones we frequently complain about when we rail against red tape.

It is safe to say that not many enjoy testifying at legislative hearings. Citizens put up with the time it takes and the stress it provokes because they are speaking on behalf of something important to them. And as a general rule, they can expect to be treated with respect, or at least indifference. This is less true for the representatives of administrative agencies. Legislators may see them as part of the problem the hearing is trying to address. At a minimum, they are expected to present appropriate information and substantive answers to the questions legislators pose.

Many legislators come to a hearing prepared not to trust what agency representatives tell them. This is understandable since agencies sometimes try to provide as little information as possible. The result can be trouble for the person testifying when this inclination to be suspicious is joined with a hot-button issue, long hours of listening to testimony, and a legislator whose personality tends to be abrasive even on good days. Chandler shares an incident that tested her staff and that she was able to find a solution for. Unfortunately, such happy endings are not the rule and directors have to decide the best strategy for satisfying the committee's demands while protecting their staff and themselves from abuse.

During the legislative session, the administrators of state agencies spend the vast majority of their time preparing for hearings and testifying or, more accurately, sitting in hearings. Top priority for the agency heads is the administration's bills and budget. Each director works hard at getting these bills heard, passed, and moved to the other legislative chamber. Usually, these bills are heard at least once. Failing to do this is seen as poor work on the part of the agency director. Legislative hearings are the time when the public has the opportunity to discuss pending bills with legislators and comment on them. This actually takes place in some committees, but the details are rarely worked out publicly.

While most legislators see their role as policymakers and are determined to remain at the policy or macro level, others see themselves as fix-it people who can push an agency into solving a problem for one of their constituents (aka a vote). Agency people may get a bit miffed when the constituent doesn't have his or her story straight or hasn't followed the rules and regulations. In addition, an administrator may not know the specifics of the particular case, and challenging the constituent during a hearing or in front of a committee would be considered rude.

At times, a legislative hearing can get quite brutal. I can recall a Senate Ways and Means Committee hearing in which two DHS staffers—both experienced, knowledgeable, and dedicated civil servants with many years of work in public service—were brought to tears. Rattling the testifiers in a public forum seemed to be the intent of the legislator. Since she was the chair, other committee members could not intervene and stop the harassment even if they had wanted to. Her questions were sometimes impossible to answer and berating, oftentimes repetitive, and seemingly designed to harass the exhausted testifier. I was relatively new to this type of legislative hearing, but eventually I moved up to the testifier's chair and told the staffers to return to DHS. Due to my role and position, I had assumed that the legislator would not treat me as badly. I was surprised to be taken to task in quite a harsh manner, but the level of harassment declined. I subsequently spoke to the governor about our unprofessional treatment, and he advised me to call the senator and explain in private that these staff members would not be testifying at any more of her hearings. In my conversation with her, I firmly told her that from this point on, I would provide all required testimony in front of her committee and any questions I could not answer would be addressed in writing at a later date.

This seemed to work because DHS staff continued to testify in front of the House Finance Committee, and these committee members remarked that they were getting a lot of excellent information. The chair of the Senate committee, while never quite apologizing, subsequently suggested that I invite my staff to her hearings as audience members in case I needed their expertise. Thus, she demonstrated respect for their expertise and indirectly agreed not to harass them. While staff and directors in the executive branch need to be deferential to the elected officials, they do not have to suffer verbal abuse. That is not part of their job descriptions.

Sometimes legislators hear a serious concern from a constituent and, perhaps to show that they are responsive, ask the agency director to come to their office for a one-on-one meeting. One senator used to do this quite frequently. Once I was called into his office to meet a constituent who had been complaining about noise and parking problems at a house next to his. Both the constituent and the legislator believed that this large house was used either for a drug rehabilitation program or a rehabilitation program for parolees. They were sure that some governmental agency was responsible for the problems and needed to be held accountable. I tried to explain that if it was indeed a substance-abuse treatment facility, it would be under the auspices of DOH and that DHS did not contract out for such programs. If it were a program for parolees, it would be the responsibility of the Department of Public Safety. If the two would give me the address of the home,

I offered, I would look it up under the state's procurement list and see which agency should be contacted. This was really the only thing I could do since I had very little information to work with. At first, the constituent didn't want to give the address (in fact, I don't think he knew it), and the house turned out not to be next door but elsewhere in his neighborhood. Nonetheless, I offered to check into such programs in the neighborhood. After quite a bit of effort, I found that there were no such state programs in that neighborhood and the large house was a private, single-family home. I sent the information to the senator, and he wanted me to meet again with the constituent. I did and suggested that the neighbors call the police when there was excessive noise. I also suggested that the police could check to see if there was a zoning violation of more than five unrelated persons sharing a house in a residential neighborhood. Without ducking the issue, I did mention that the police were under the jurisdiction of the city and county and not the state. I thought I was being quite helpful, but evidently this was not satisfactory to this legislator. He took it upon himself to talk about this issue on the floor of the Senate during my reconfirmation hearing and voted against me, citing my apparent unresponsiveness to his constituent's problem. It is simply not possible to please everyone.

Some legislators attempt to amend a statute to fix a constituent's problem. When this happens, the resulting legislation usually becomes extraordinarily detailed. If passed, it is often impossible for the agency to implement. Later, when an agency may want to correct or amend even the smallest change in the statute, another bill must be drafted, which results in more hearings and a new cycle. Every change, no matter how small, must be introduced by

> In the health and human services field, many consumers and clients attend the hearings and have specific, sometimes very specific, concerns and complaints. Hawai'i has a wonderfully open and accessible legislative process that encourages citizens to come and testify. Some legislators see themselves as advocates for their constituents and attempt to solve problems on the spot during a hearing rather than remain at the policy-setting level. Legislators may get quite involved in an individual person's testimony. For example, a consumer may say, "No one has helped me find a job," and in order to be responsive to his or her constituent, a legislator may ask the welfare division administrator to join the legislator's table and then grill her on why the agency hasn't found this person a job.

a legislator and is referred to the appropriate committee (and a money committee if there is an appropriation attached, or the judiciary committee if there are legal implications). It must pass all the committees and be approved by the entire chamber—a process repeated by the other chamber. Most bills do not pass, so these kinds of administrative changes are not likely to make it through a session.

Administrative rules are much easier to create or amend than statutes, and there are hearings at which the public may testify. However, when a legislator wants to fix things for good, he or she amends the statute, leaving very little flexibility for the agency. There seems to be tension between legislators writing laws with broad policy language (the agencies prefer this) and those who use such detail in their legislation that it is like administrative rules, which the agencies must obey. When there is a good relationship between the agency staff and the legislators and when the agency is responsive to a legislator's call about a constituent's complaint, this tension may be minimized.

11 | Community Advocates; or, It Is So Much Easier to Advocate Than Administrate

Issues that look one way to administrative agencies with the responsibility for certain public mandates can look another way to community groups that see these issues as relevant to themselves. In many ways, these relations are like those between landlords and tenants. Tension and conflict are almost inevitable because their perspectives and interests are so different.

At the same time, it is evident that in many ways these relationships are at the heart of our notions of democracy. Making them work as well as possible is critical to democracy's success. Their importance raises a number of questions. How do we better inform the public about what agencies are doing so that their responses to the work of those agencies are more useful? How do we make people in these bureaucracies more willing to involve the public in their work? Putting these together, how can we create a more consultative and deliberative relationship between agencies and their publics? Some believe the increase in e-government and open technology will improve the flow of information and ease the public's access to agency data. This may be true, but it needs to be accompanied by changes in the orientation and skills of agency personnel and a real-world understanding among community agencies and citizens of how such systems work.

Advocates are in the enviable position of never having to be accountable for the administration of the program for which they advocate. This instantly structures the debate (and conflict) between the public agency and the community. Legislators play a role in the middle. Citizens often have only a vague idea about how to make the things they want actually happen. Community activists therefore tend to push their issues and desires into the laps of legislators when they could be working more closely with an agency and, for example, advocating for more money to expand services or programs. There is a significant lack of trust between advocates and bureaucrats. Advocates often have seen that the only way to get an agency to change is to push very hard and, when in doubt, try to get legislation to force change. While at times this works, it often is heavy handed, polarizing, and not necessarily good strategy.

For example, a person may go to a public hearing and complain to legislators about an individual case when the authority for that decision resides at the judiciary. Or a mother may come to a hearing and complain about CPS when, in fact, it is family court that made the decision to terminate her parental rights. Or an advocate may complain about treatment a client received and about which no one at the hearing has any independent information. Often the director is called to the table to answer why something happened to Ms. Y, but the director has no prior information about the case or the circumstance. At times the situation is not even under his or her agency's control. Confidentiality prevents any staff person from talking about the specifics of any case, so these hearings tend to be frustrating places to try to problem solve. People frequently complain to the director of an agency about a statutorily mandated requirement that the legislature passed. Banging on the wrong door usually is ineffective.

Another example is the placement of the Executive Office on Aging (EOA). This is an office with a strong citizen advisory board and a powerful constituency. Perhaps because many of these advocates are retired and passionate about issues on aging, they take the time to become active at the legislature, monitoring bills and testifying at hearings throughout the session. The EOA for many years was attached to the governor's office. Its director, board, staff, and advocates liked this as it gave them close access to the governor along with a certain amount of prestige. However, it was unconstitutional for a line agency to be inside the governor's office, so several attempts were made to move it to a state agency, all meeting fierce resistance.

Governor Cayetano decided that since it programmatically fit within the very broad mandate of DHS, it should go there as an attached agency. EOA would remain semi-autonomous and retain its own executive director. This action needed legislative approval, and with the attorney general testifying the move was necessary to prevent a loss of federal funds, the bill passed. The EOA advocates then went to work to move the office out of DHS. Their concern was that DHS was a poor people's agency and the mission of the EOA was to help all seniors remain active, healthy, and socially engaged; support family caregivers; and ensure that Hawai'i's communities had the necessary economy, workforce, and physical capacity for an aging society. In short, there was concern that if EOA was attached to DHS, even for administrative purposes, it would be stigmatized by being associated with needy persons. EOA recommended that it be placed with DOH.

While this may have been seen as just another turf war, there were good reasons for placement inside DHS. Adult Protective Services, Medicaid's Home and Community Based Services for elderly and disabled persons, job training, vocational rehabilitation and services for the blind, food stamps, and social security disability determinations were all at DHS. Many seniors were already getting services from one or more of these programs. Logic did not prevail. While I was away for my two-week vacation, the governor's chief of staff agreed to introduce legislation to relocate EOA to DOH.

Often I met privately with individual legislators to encourage them to refer complainants back to the agency. And while a director rarely has time to spend with individual client complaints, it actually may save time in the long run (and provide a better resolution for a client) if advocates and even individual clients meet with the director first, before going to a public hearing. It is clear that no one but the director will satisfy the person or persons with concerns, even though another staff person in the agency may be better informed about the rules and the individual situation. I set up a Financial Assistance Advisory Committee, affectionately known as FAAC, in order to try to get input from consumers, advocates, and the public about problems they were having with the agency. My intent was not only to learn about the problems, but also to try to avoid these discussions at the legislature.

On health and human services issues, the advocates and the legislators on the subject committee want the agency to do more, but they rarely can find any additional funds to allocate to the agency's budget. The debates usually take a form in which the community groups and the legislators complain that not enough is being done, or not in the right ways, while the agency defends itself with "We don't have the staff, the money, the information system, *yada, yada, yada*." Saying that we have other priorities to an advocate group is seen as unresponsive and may be interpreted as an adversarial stance. This may cause more serious problems later on in terms of garnering community support when the agency needs it to protect programs against budget cuts or to expand programs.

It is crucial for the delivery of high-quality public sector services to improve the understanding about this work to the community at large, and vice versa. The communication barriers between the public sector and the private sector (usually the nonprofit organizations) may result in unnecessary turf battles, inefficiencies, duplication, and gaps in the provision of services. Often there are legislative information briefings in the months between sessions that are designed to bring organizations, advocates, and the public sector together to hammer out solutions. Finding better forms of communication is advisable. DHS organized many advisory boards and groups at the division level as well as at the director's level to solicit input and build relationships with consumers, advocates, and professionals.

12 | The Governor: or, The Guy Who Holds the Purse Strings

Chandler begins here by observing that the Hawai'i governor has a lot of power. This is true in comparison to other states. It is also the case that the Hawai'i governor's influence over the budget is a major source of that power. At the same time, it is also true that in many ways the governor has little power. Chandler illustrates that here with the problem of downsizing. It is very difficult and politically costly if the governor tries to reduce the number of public sector employees. For example, union negotiations have given people whose jobs have been cut the option of bumping employees with less seniority. Because this includes employees in other departments, bumping can create organizational chaos. The larger questions here are about the dynamics of downsizing, something notoriously difficult to do in the private sector as well. Should it be across the board, in which every agency suffers more or less equally? Or should it be targeted, in which case specific units are selected for reduction or elimination? If cuts are necessary, how should the governor make them? By depending on the professional expertise of his cabinet appointments? On that of external consultants? On data? On politics? How should the governor and his directors handle the stress this places on cooperation among and within departments? And what has to be done to ensure that cuts produce greater organizational efficiency rather than organizational decay?

Chandler also makes reference to the fact that Hawai'i has both an extensive civil service system and unionized public employees. It is hard to know which of these is more powerful in terms of the day-to-day operations of agencies and the relationships between appointed officials and agency personnel. What is certain is that the two together can make any changes to programs and personnel challenging.

As the chief executive officer in Hawai'i, the governor has a lot of power. The governor controls the budget and therefore the actions of his or her departments. The governor may elect to veto line items in the legislative budget, not spend appropriated monies, or restrict appropriations. Since the governor may choose not to allocate the money that has been appropriated by the legislature, he or she has the power to direct dollars where desired.

Is that all ya got?

The governor is the agency director's boss. In Hawai'i, there are sixteen cabinet agencies and the governor leads and manages all of them. This can be especially difficult when resources are scarce. The state budget, by constitutional amendment, must balance; there can be no deficit. When tax revenues are flowing in, it is easy to maintain or increase current services. When they are not, it is a nightmare! When tax revenues are down, the governor generally requests from each department budget-cutting scenarios detailing the impact of a two-percent, five-percent or ten-percent cut. Usually this is accompanied by such instructions as maintain the core functions of government, do not distress the public, do not lay off staff, and do not hire anybody nonessential. After the first few rounds of cuts, this becomes quite difficult or even impossible. The governor must listen to each director's proposal and then choose from among the options. Inevitably, this sets up a competition among the cabinet members, and people assume that those with the best access to the governor (e.g., those who get meetings scheduled easily) fare better.

The governor must balance the state budget according to the projections of the statutorily created Council on Revenues. The council issues quarterly reports that predict what the next quarter's tax revenues will be. Agencies often gamble by spending more money than has been appropriated in the first quarter with the hope that additional revenues will flow in during the subsequent quarters and the governor's restrictions will be removed before the end of the fiscal year.

Another ploy is for directors to propose an extreme cut to a very popular program and present this as the only option. The assumption is that the governor won't cut a popular program and will have to look to another agency. While this may be strategic for the proposing agency, it is not a cooperative strategy and does not serve the governor (or the community) well.

Predicting future revenues makes it difficult for the governor to manage since not only do the tax revenues fluctuate widely month to month but so does the number of people in need of government services. Compounding the problem is the fact that use of government services varies inversely. For example, as revenues and jobs decrease, the need for food stamps, housing, and medical care increases; that is, more people become eligible for these services as their family incomes decrease. Thus, DHS has more clients to assist as the economy gets worse, but is given no additional staff. In a worst-case scenario, even DHS will face budget cuts.

The larger agencies are better able to tolerate budget cuts and hiring freezes than the smaller ones. Departments with large federal budgets often are protected. The smaller agencies have an extremely hard time defining their mission as essential since the bigger ones (DOE, DHS, and DOH) have large numbers of constituents who go to the legislature and complain. This noise gets translated into legislative priorities that make it harder for the governor to reduce appropriations to these agencies.

The governor may wish to protect the agencies that provide the most essential services, but most—read "all"—see their services as essential. If the number of warm bodies cannot be reduced, how can department budgets be cut? Approximately seventy percent of the state's budget is spent on employee wages and benefits. Tightening the belt can become the pattern year after year. One thousand little budget cuts actually prevent innovation, deter automation and modernization, and make government *less* efficient. Eventually, less gets done. Falling revenue results in the governor being frustrated since his or her new initiatives cannot be implemented and everyone just seems to be hanging on, waiting for an upturn in the economy. This is not a good way to run a railroad, or get reelected.

It is interesting to consider whether the inverse equation is true. That is, would innovation, automation, and efficiencies abound in a government with more money? Maybe not, but it is extremely hard for improvements to occur with falling budgets and a policy that prohibits closing programs or making significant reductions in staff. In regard to layoffs and position shifting, the public sector unions in Hawai'i are strong and have built a formidable seniority system. The Democratic Party has been a strong supporter of labor, and government has been a large employer in the state. It is extremely difficult to shift gears and make programmatic changes once civil service personnel have been hired. More recently, non–civil service or exempt positions have been created that presumably will give the public agencies more flexibility. However, these appointments or hires may also be more partisan and the people less qualified, as we have seen during President Bush's administration and now the Obama administration. At the same time, these temporary positions provide less security and this makes vacant positions difficult to fill.

13 | The Cabinet; or, When Collaboration Seems Like…Getting Clobbered

Governor's cabinets are made up of individuals, each successful in his or her own right, who find themselves asked to be both team members and high-stakes competitors. They are members of a team whose purpose is to advance the governor's agenda. They are also competitors who want to promote and protect the interests of their departments, as well as their own political and professional opportunities. The tension between cooperating and competing is not unique to this setting, but because the stakes are high, balance is especially difficult to achieve.

Cabinets play different roles in administrations, depending on the personality of the elected leader, his or her relationships with cabinet members, and their relationships with one another. Some governors use the cabinet mainly as a place to announce policy or describe how the administration is going to deal with a specific situation. When the cabinet is used this way, a secondary group of department heads may be created, formally or informally, to provide advice to the elected leader. If a governor uses the cabinet as a consultative body, then some members will become more influential than others. Their influence will depend on their personalities, their relationships with the elected leader, and the size and status of the departments they head.

One might expect that agency directors' need for the governor's (or legislators') attention would be served by a rational process, but it isn't. Like sibling rivalry, this process is often a zero-sum game. If DOH is being protected from cuts, every other agency must be cut more deeply to balance the state budget. While the goal may be interagency cooperation and presentation of a united front, directors quickly become advocates for their own agencies and thus less cooperative and collaborative.

The governor's chief of staff tries to work out disputes among the cabinet agencies. However, solving problems among ambitious equals when the stakes are high is extremely difficult.

Governor Cayetano's cabinet was composed of all the executive branch department heads, the lieutenant governor, the superintendent of DOE, the UH president, the governor's chief of staff, and members of the governor's office. (The DOE superintendent was not invited to cabinet meetings during the Lingle administration.) In the early days of the Cayetano administration, the cabinet met weekly throughout the legislative session. The governor always ran the meetings and was clearly the person in charge. The topics most often discussed were the governor's legislative agenda at the capitol and the state budget. The B&F director was usually asked to report on the grim budget situation. Then the governor would direct us to be creative in finding places to make cuts.

The governor also initiated several attempts to bring the cabinet together to work on a common vision. Business consultants from the private sector, team builders, coalition coaches, reinventors of government, and privatizing experts were hired to train the cabinet directors…but they were not very successful. While training was helpful for some directors—those who learned and practiced new skills within their agencies—these sessions did not get the directors to work better with each other.

A number of inter-departmental budget meetings were held to define what were to be considered *core* functions of government and to clarify what each department was actually doing. There were attempts to find out who had nonessential programs or services that might be reduced or deleted. Each director had to work within the confines of federal and state mandate, consumer or constituency interest group, union and civil service rules of seniority, and staff resistance. Most of the directors resorted to making deals with the governor on an individual basis. Sub-cabinet or cross-cabinet initiatives sound great, but were unsuccessful, at least in this administration, in solving serious budget problems. Eventually, the governor had to make the hard decisions and probably did this independently of cabinet members.

Coordination and Tension among Departments; or, If These Are Your Friends…

While Hawai'i was still a territory, statehood advocates believed, with considerable justification, that they needed to demonstrate a commitment to democratic practices and the capacity to form and run an effective government. With this as motivation, a model constitution was drafted in 1950 that contained the then-current principles of good government. Among these principles was the creation of a small number of independent, cabinet-level departments.

As the following section makes clear, the constitutional principle did not solve the question for all time, and the debate about the number of departments and their relations continues. Agencies evolve in response to requests from the legislature to take on new responsibilities, the missions of successive administrations, and desires for larger budgets and more staff. As agencies evolve, they incorporate overlapping functions, and from an outsider's perspective, it often is not clear who is doing what or how the entire structure is supposed to work. There have been proposals to consolidate agencies or to create a superagency within which all of the functions can be placed. Such a superagency might meet the need for administrative coordination, but over time, if not in the beginning, it could suffer from lack of a clear mission. The federal Department of Homeland Security is an excellent example of this.

Hawai'i's state constitution limits the number of executive-level cabinet departments to nineteen (including the DOE, the UH, which has a board of regents, and the Office of Hawaiian Affairs, which has elected directors). There has been discussion about expanding this number, which would require a constitutional amendment, to add a department of the environment. (An office of the environment currently sits in DOH, but many legislators feel it should be promoted to cabinet-level status.) Other proposed agencies include a long-term-care department, a substance abuse department, a children and youth department, and even a military affairs department. Now people may be discussing the need for a homeland security department. The hope held out for a new cabinet-level agency is that it will better coordinate the activities of the many agencies whose overlapping mandates lead to fragmentation and duplication.

Some states tinker with the design of agencies in an attempt to get better organizational structures and coordination. In Hawai'i, an example of a service that has been the subject of reorganization discussion is the Developmental Disabilities Division in DOH, which manages the Medicaid Waiver program. The division's services are designed by DOH but funded with Medicaid dollars that are managed by DHS. This separation of functions makes coordination quite challenging. There have been both legislative and administrative efforts to simplify this complex organizational structure. However, each department feels that it is doing a good job and therefore opposes any consolidation.

At one time, consultants were hired by each side to mediate. One consultant from another state, paid for by DOH, advised DHS to just send

DOH's bills to the federal government and hope for reimbursement, even though the experts at DHS believed that some expenditures were inappropriate. "What is the worst thing that can happen?" the consultant asked. In fact, the worst thing that had been anticipated actually happened: the federal government did not reimburse the state for a bill submitted by DOH, and the bill had to be paid by DHS.

The "Service" Departments; or, Hey! Aren't We on the Same Team?

In the title for this section, the word "service" is in quotes to suggest that those who are the recipients of the work of these departments often do not see themselves served. Service, or support, departments perform three broad functions in the public sector: they handle personnel matters, they organize the budget, and they buy services and equipment.

Relations between line departments—those departments that deal directly with different segments of the public—and service departments are often tense. The line departments think that they know their own needs and should be allowed to meet them. Service departments believe that without coordination and oversight, the system would be out of control. As Chandler illustrates with the drama of the toilet-paper dispenser, the result can be a lot of time spent jockeying for position. In this jockeying, the departments seek ways to get things done without being penalized by the central agencies. People who are good at this are invaluable resources.

In recent years it has become popular to talk about decentralization—devolving to the line departments some of the things that the service departments currently do. A key area is personnel, for which departments would like more flexibility and speed in taking action. This has been accompanied in Hawai'i by calls to consolidate the service departments themselves. Not much of this has happened to date. As Chandler's experience suggests, tensions between support and line agencies, and creative efforts to resolve them, are likely to continue.

In Hawai'i, B&F is responsible for proposing a budget for the governor that is in balance each year. This means that B&F must beat the agencies into submission to get the numbers to "work." One strategy of the budget staff seemed to be to request more and more justifications for establishing new positions, filling old positions, approving travel requests…even buying paperclips. When approvals are required at many levels within the system, it automatically, and often by design, slows down the agency's spending. Staffers become so discouraged that many requests are not written up because it is so hard to get an approval. This strategy may indeed save a few dollars when deficits loom, but it is not the best way to administer public programs. Perseverance is rewarded, not necessarily good planning or budgeting.

The Department of Accounting and General Services (DAGS) is another agency that has interesting relationships with the line agencies. DAGS staff processes the checks for all personnel, purchase orders, and contracts; is responsible for all leases; and basically oversees all agency purchases. It never, ever releases funds until the paperwork is perfect. Sometimes its regulations seemed a bit excessive to me. For example, when I was presented with my first one hundred contracts, DAGS included two forms for each contract requiring my signature. The contracts exempted the provider from civil serv-

This is streamlining?

ice requirements. I refused to waste my time on this mind-numbing and unnecessary task. I asked my staff to prepare a form with my signature already on it, and I would date each to make the review fresh. Nope! DAGS said, "This cannot be done. The director must sign using black ink on each and every copy." I was told that DAGS would not issue the contracts and, even worse, the providers would not be paid if I didn't sign. If true, this would be a serious consequence.

So I called the director of DAGS. She said she needed to talk to the AG. We all met to search for a solution. While they were sympathetic to my aching hand, they would not agree to change the rule nor introduce legislation to make a change. They suggested I introduce legislation, which I subsequently did. After much effort, new legislation was passed to slightly modify the cumbersome procedure.

Clearly this type of change should not need legislative or public deliberation and should be addressed through administrative rules, not statute. Interestingly enough, for several months after my complaints, I didn't see any contracts. For a while I thought I had solved the problem. However, it turned out my deputy director had agreed to sign these forms (my signature could be delegated to her, but only her), and she was doing it to skirt the problem and resolve any interagency disputes that I might have been causing. In my model of line-support agency relationships, I would have expected the support agency to help *solve* this problem.

This next example, while humorous, also illustrates the effort that a line agency must make to bring about a change being resisted by a support agency. From my first day on the job it was annoying to go to the ladies' restroom on our floor since the building had an old-style toilet-paper dispenser. This was the type usually found in elementary schools. It was shaped like a small box and had a small slot in the bottom in which individual pieces of paper were folded and stacked. Most of the experienced staff knew that ninety-nine times out of one hundred the paper didn't come out the bottom. They knew to bring keys or a nail file into the bathroom to dislodge the stuck toilet paper.

This became a leadership challenge! I asked the DHS administrative officer to request a new toilet-paper dispenser from DAGS, not only for the women's restroom, but for the men's restroom as well (never to be called sexist). In a fit of collaboration we also requested new dispensers for the

One step for womankind.

entire building so that DOE, which shares the Liliu'okalani Building with DHS, would benefit from this organizational improvement.

"Can't do it" was the reply. This escalated into a serious issue. DAGS rejected our request to change the dispensers because they reasoned that staff and visitors might steal toilet paper rolls and take them home. For six years we requested and, each time, were denied. Finally, as part of my birthday celebration there was a wonderful surprise. The creative DHS deputy director convinced the administrative officer, who had been half-heartedly sending over requests for a new toilet-paper dispenser, to actually install a plastic dispenser himself. It also came with a twenty-four toilet-paper pack from Costco. The stall's sign read "Susan's Place for the Day," and the stall was reserved for the director as a birthday gift. Perhaps the funniest part of the surprise was that the administrative officer said a bit sheepishly, "Susan, you know that this hasn't been approved by DAGS." Probably to this day it hasn't.

The point here is that working through the existing system of line and support relationships can be tedious and tiresome. While respecting the expertise of these agencies, particularly personnel and budgetary services, at times the line agency needs to find creative, yet legal, ways around the rules and requirements when the benefit is clearly to the agency and its operations (and, even more importantly, to the clients it serves).

While all state agencies are established to serve the public, some are more focused on following rules—like the Department of Human Resource Development (DHRD)—ensuring that people being hired have been recruited and selected fairly. B&F often needs to find money from other agencies, like DOH, DHS, and DOE. These agencies deal more directly with the public and have a mission to be as responsive as possible.

There have been many recommendations to address these line-support issues. Some suggest that the staff functions—like personnel, administrative services, budget—should be consolidated, therefore flattening and streamlining the many approval levels. Others think that a line agency needs to have greater authority and responsibility over its basic operations. While there is great expertise in the support agencies, like B&F or DHRD, their focus seems to be on checking and rechecking other levels of work (and other agencies' work) before making a decision and advancing an issue for the governor's approval. This intentionally (or unintentionally) slows the decision-making process. Transferring some of the expertise to the line agencies for routine operations would be helpful and increase efficiency. It is important to note, however, that these interagency spats also occurred internally, with the line departments expressing similar frustration with their internal support offices. Perhaps due to their differing organizational vantage points, it is hard to see the issues the same way. Teams made up of employees from the line and support agencies were able at times to strategize and problem solve on specific issues. This worked internally as well at DHS.

For example, employees in the divisions, particularly in child protection and benefits, were quite vocal about criticizing the department personnel office. The complaint was primarily about the length of time it took the department to recruit and hire new staff. Especially when a vacant position could easily get lost by getting swept away by either the governor or the legislature, it was risky to delay hiring someone for six months while waiting for a piece of paper documenting that he or she had graduated from UH last May—a university that was literally less than five miles away. Perhaps a phone call would have sufficed? The personnel office felt besieged by requests to hurry up. Sometimes the requests were to revise a position description or minimum qualifications. Sometimes the DHS personnel office needed to get approvals from DHRD for things as minor as changing questions on a recruitment interview form. The line staff wanted to take control of these personnel matters and believed they could fill their vacancies faster. This was important because vacant positions cause morale problems since caseloads are heavier with less staff. However, personnel rules and regulations are quite complex and, if applied incorrectly, may lead to hiring unqualified staff or the filing of time-consuming grievances.

One advantage of outsourcing a project is that the private sector has a much easier method of hiring and firing staff. While the private sector employees often don't have the protections of unionized civil servants, at times a department can get so fed up with the delays, rules, and regulations of the state system that it can decide not to hire a public sector worker. This is not a good situation.

14 | The Auditor; or, Uh-Oh, Here She Comes Again!

The Office of the Legislative Auditor was established to help the legislature with its responsibility to oversee the work of the administrative agencies. Although individual legislators can tell the auditor what they would like examined, the work of the agency is considered to be independent of the legislature. The maintenance of this balance between serving the needs of the legislature and remaining independent and nonpartisan is crucial to the auditor's credibility.

The concerns raised by Chandler about the auditor's work are not about partisanship or political agenda, but about the way the audits are prepared. It is entirely predictable that agencies whose work is being carefully scrutinized will complain about the process in order to avoid having to take seriously the issues raised in the audit. At the same time, it is worth recognizing that there are lots of opportunities for things to go wrong. These include the audit appearing to extend beyond its mandate, the agency being audited appearing to withhold information, and too little of the final report being given to highlighting successes and too much to exposing mistakes.

To the extent that Chandler's concerns are shared by other agencies, the usefulness of the audits—that is, the extent to which what is learned will be used to improve things—is undermined. This would be important at any time, but it could become more significant in the future. If reforms in the public sector give agencies more flexibility with which to do their work, then it follows that there will be a corresponding need for more effective systems of oversight and accountability.

A legislative audit in Hawaiʻi is synonymous with stress and anxiety for people in public sector agencies. Most state agencies dread visits from the auditor because there is a long history of adversarial relationships between that agency and the state's departments. The trouble usually begins when the legislature passes a resolution requesting a legislative audit of a department or program. Often the resolution's purpose is unclear and the scope unmanageable. The large agencies already have federal audits and other annual managerial and fiscal audits, so another poorly framed one from the legislature is seen as time consuming and not particularly helpful.

Most public sector employees believe that there has never been an agency that the auditor liked. The auditor's reports are usually quite critical. Often the auditor makes suggestions that the agency itself had offered but doesn't have the funds to implement. Or the agency believes it has already made the suggested changes by the time the audit is published. The agency never really gets a chance to correct an audit report since the auditor's materials and worksheets are confidential. If an agency complains that the data are inaccurate or incorrect, there is no requirement that the auditor show how the data were collected or what the findings were based on. The media love the "Gotcha!" mentality of the audits and seem happy to save space for negative findings. The agencies look weak when responding, "We made those changes already" or "We don't know how the auditor came up with those findings." The best strategy seems to be to humbly say, "Thank you, Ma'am… We're working on it." An auditor's report should help an agency since the criticisms usually come with a clear need for change and/or for money, which hopefully the legislature will provide. But most often the criticisms simply sting and bring bad press. Money to fix the problems rarely follows. Agencies are subsequently viewed by the public as inept and wasting taxpayers' money.

Legislators seem to feel that they cannot get sufficient information from the agencies, so they often work under the assumption that the agency is hiding money or spending it inappropriately. Our lawmakers like to direct the auditor to focus on the agency but rarely for the benefit of the agency or the legislators. The auditor's staff is not required to cost out its recommendations, so it may suggest after a DHS audit that, for example, all child protection cases should be reviewed by a supervisor before a CPS worker refers them to another unit. After evaluating the recommendation, DHS would respond that putting the expensive procedure in place would require additional staff and create an extensive delay in case processing. Yet these recommendations become big news in the media and can result in subsequent legislative hearings to discuss the auditor's suggestions. With no money allocated to implement such changes, this becomes an exercise in futility and frustration for the staff and the director's office.

Federal audits and those conducted by professional auditing firms usually have a specific time frame and a clearly defined scope. These auditors talk to the agency staff and discuss how to obtain the necessary data to produce an accurate analysis. Before the final audit report is issued, there are exit interviews with the staff so that unusual or unexpected findings can be discussed. Staff members are provided the opportunity to further explain agency processes, and there is time to respond and suggest corrective action strategies before the report is publicized. A considerable number of beneficial recommendations come out of these focused audits.

I would suggest that the legislative auditor include recommendations such as cost estimates, statutory or rule changes, and even implementation strategies in these final reports. This may require expertise and resources that the legislative auditor's office doesn't have. However, changing the audits so that they analyze an agency's strengths and weaknesses would be more beneficial to the agency and to the legislature. Agency audits have the potential to help a department unearth problems in such areas as accounting or information systems and help formulate realistic, corrective action plans. Auditors can also inform agencies about other states' efforts with similar programs, which is very helpful.

I found it amusing to observe that Governor Lingle's departments had the same types of problems as Cayetano's. Their message has changed from "Let the auditor get in there to expose waste, fraud, and abuse" to "The auditor doesn't seem to fully understand the programs and the good work of our staff."

15 | The Press; or, the Unkindest Cut of All…

The relationship between government agencies and the media is often difficult. One of Chandler's proposals is to better equip public officials for their encounters with the media by giving them training. The case of the Hawai'i van-cam fiasco, which she mentions, is a good example of when such training may have been beneficial to the public. Although it is true that part of the problem was the media's need to sensationalize the issue, a contributing factor was the inability of the public agency spokesperson to deal effectively with the questions that were coming from citizens and, soon thereafter, legislators.

Training may be helpful, but Chandler's concerns raise larger issues. The media's business-driven need to reduce issues to their simplest and most dramatic elements is a threat to the need of citizens for realistic understanding of issues that are complex. It is also a threat to the healthy dialogue that needs to go on between citizens and the public agencies that attempt to work on their behalf.

The media play a crucial role in public policy formation. Their understanding often shapes the public's support or opposition. If a newspaper, radio, or television station gets interested in an issue, it can make or break the matter. The media often can keep an issue alive or deep-six it. Emotionally charged issues like putting cameras in mobile vans for nabbing speeders (aka Van-Cam), or a vicious child abuse case, may stay in the headlines for months before they run their course.

The governor, legislators, and affected state agencies are required to repeat their positions over and over again for the various media outlets. The media frequently force public officials to keep responding, keep explaining, and keep describing a policy to the point that they get a bit testy and seem defensive. This of course is the sound bite the press loves best. Conflict sells papers and leads the television news cycles.

The newspapers and television do an excellent job of putting a face to a tragedy. For example, they can humanize a problem like crystal methamphetamine abuse by talking to families and individuals who know firsthand what the drug can do. The media often can set up a story for the community to think about so that when the legislators get interested there has been some background work already done. This is positive and important in a democracy. However, the media also can get their teeth into a story that is very emotional but not very significant in terms of public effect.

In retrospect, many in the governor's cabinet felt that the Department of Transportation (DOT) was getting a bum rap, mostly because it was not able to get its case about the van-cam program out clearly to the community. Most of the departments in the Cayetano administration had no press or information officer. This was probably a mistake. When the media call an agency, they want to talk to the department director. The governor wanted each director to respond to any and all press requests within twenty-four hours. If a particular director was uncomfortable with the press, or not very good at answering questions in digestible chunks, that lack of media savvy became a big problem for the department and the governor. With a large and complex bureaucracy like DHS, a question such as "Why did this agency move this child from a foster home?" may take the director twenty-four hours just to identify the case.

Nonetheless, the directors were told by the governor never to say, "No

---

The van-cam experiment case is an interesting example. A bill was passed by the legislature that empowered DOT to contract for ninety days with a private firm to take a radar-activated picture from a van parked on the side of the roadway of a vehicle that was allegedly speeding. The speeder would eventually receive a ticket in the mail along with visual evidence of the violation.

Programs in several states had been implemented successfully, but in Hawai'i, a few legislators, the talk-radio network, television stations, and newspapers began ranting about the proposed permanent bill. Radio and television stations day after day had callers alarmed that "Big Brother" would be looking into their cars. Many public commentators did not accurately describe how the statute was written or would be implemented. However, the public began raising concerns that an unsuspecting car owner would suddenly be thrown in jail if someone else was driving the car and was caught on camera speeding. Many important issues were being discussed at the legislature in that session, but this one took centerstage and was front-page news for weeks. Governor Cayetano ordered the experimental program halted on April 10, 2002, a day before the legislature voted to repeal the law establishing the use of the cameras.

---

comment," and were encouraged to answer the questions quickly and fully. Few of the directors had any public relations training, and often this showed. It is extremely important for public sector administrators to have effective communication skills and the ability, as well as the knowledge, to inform the public about their agency's operations. It would be a good idea for a director to get press and media training before taking such a public job. Even on-the-job training would have been helpful.

I instituted the policy at DHS that only the director or the deputy director should talk to the media. Some agencies would refer them to a division administrator, but at DHS I kept a pretty tight control on the message. The primary reason for this was to make sure that the director knew what issues were emerging and not be caught off guard. No director, or governor, likes to be caught off guard about something that happened in his or her agency by reading about it in the newspaper or seeing an employee on television describing breaking events. Worse yet is seeing a quote from someone within the department that is a complete surprise to the director. Surprising the governor was also a very big and serious no-no. Providing easy access to the media was crucial to ensuring the public understood the department's position on an event or issue. DHS understood the need for television reporters to file reports by 4 p.m. for the 5 or 6 p.m. newscast, and we tried to accommodate that schedule.

My background in education led me to assume that the media really were interested in learning the details of a program or policy. To my dismay this was not always the case. The newspaper and television reporters who do human-interest stories are often the youngest and most inexperienced in the business. Some said they were in purgatory, doing time while waiting to get onto some solid stories. Few took the time to understand a multi-layered story fully, and often the submitted story would get edited to the point where even they were embarrassed by what was aired or ended up in print. Others had their own idea of the story and basically just wanted your picture to round out their piece.

The media are not necessarily the best places to educate the public about complex public issues. The storyline has to be short, juicy, and, if at all possible, controversial. If something is happening in the department that meets these needs, you are popular; otherwise, getting important public information out through the media is extremely hard.

16 | The Federal Presence; or, Will This Be Good for Us?

It is well known that public officials in Hawai'i, like their counterparts in other states, often have mixed feelings about the role played by federal agencies. Sometimes, such as in areas of public corruption, it brings the authority, resources, and motivation to do things the local officials cannot. Other times, as with unfunded mandates in education, health, or welfare, it can be seen as presenting problems. Local officials may feel that their federal counterparts "just don't understand us"—the political culture of Hawai'i and its orientations to social welfare.

There are less visible aspects of the federal presence: the conventional wisdom that federal monies are free, the additional burden created by being successful at getting federal monies, and the case of welfare reform. Public service takes place in the context of a political culture that is continually shifting. In the case of welfare reform, the shift of a sixty-year federal entitlement program into a block grant with extensive state, rather than federal, control requires a significant shift in programs, policies, processes, and organizational culture.

This is helpful?

The bottom line is this: federal mandates are powerful. With a mandate things are much more likely to happen at the state level. While the legislature passes hundreds of new laws each year, adding to the thousands of statutes enacted since statehood in 1959, at DHS it is the federal laws that make state employees listen up. Many of the state welfare programs and services are either funded with federal funds (like food stamps) or funded in partnership with the states (like Medicaid). Some are funded in a block grant proportional to the poverty rate of the state (like temporary assistance to needy families) with great flexibility for how the money is spent by the state, and still others are competitively awarded for a special program (like a health-care program for Native Hawaiians).

Sometimes directors use federal mandates to protect themselves against cuts from the governor or the legislature. Sometimes directors use a federal mandate to protect themselves from certain types of collaboration with other directors and agencies. A federally funded mandate (which of course is much better than an unfunded one) provides an agency with a path to follow. Even when federal rules appear vague and unclear, there are actions expected by the federal government that the funded agency must take seriously. It is not just the federal dollars that are influential, but also the *power* of the federal government that moves agencies to action.

> *The case of welfare reform is illustrative of the federal government's impact on state agencies. The new federal initiative called the Personal Responsibility and Work Opportunity Reconciliation Act of 1996 was designed to change welfare as we know it, and it did. Hawai'i, because of its cultural traditions, island economy, and special fiscal circumstances, was the only state among the fifty not reducing its welfare rolls prior to this new law. However, to outsiders, such as federal policy analysts, this looked like failure. This raises an important question about the meaning of success and underscores how tied it is to perspective.*

It is also a fact that being awarded federal funds or a block grant is like winning the lottery. It seems like free money since it didn't come from the legislature! We sometimes forget that we pay taxes to the federal government too. A state agency acquires considerable standing within the governor's administration for obtaining federal grants or bonuses, even federal funds based on straight population formulas, which of course may not be made part of the public announcement.

The legislature strongly encourages all state agencies to apply for federal funds and grants. Legislators often pass resolutions urging state agencies to hire grant writers when applying for federal funds. This sounds reasonable, but there is resistance deep within the agencies since employees know that grants are hard to obtain and, once awarded, require a tremendous amount of work to implement. Hawai'i does not have a good track record of securing competitive grants, and new programs are rarely funded adequately for the long term. Receiving a federal grant may mean more stress on the existing infrastructure. Staff members also worry that new grant money has a limited implementation period. Almost as soon as the grant arrives, there is pressure to figure out how to keep the program alive when the federal money disappears and state funds are inadequate.

The state of Hawai'i has a long history of caring for its residents. Instituting a welfare reform program that removed people from the welfare rolls or limiting cash benefits has never been done by the state legislature. Only when the federal government in 1996 *required* the states to establish five-year time limits on cash assistance and provided federal funds in a block grant appropriation did Hawai'i change its welfare programs. Even then, DHS worked with the governor and the legislature to keep a strong focus on job training, education, childcare, and support programs. DHS, along with community welfare-rights advocates, designed an assistance program that permitted attending school to count and to meet the work definition. Another innovative policy that Hawai'i put in place was the protection that when the five-year mandatory period ended for some families, they were still assured that childcare, food stamps, and Medicaid would continue through state-funded, work-support programs. This permitted families who found work, even part-time work that paid low wages, to continue to receive a cash supplement so they could get out of poverty. DHS also designed a fully state-funded program for immigrants who became ineligible for all federal assistance in the 1996 reform. These programs were funded even in the tough economic times, primarily due to the governor's strong commitment to the poor.

Some saw these programs as progressive social policy; some saw this as increasing dependency; and some felt the state didn't go far enough in helping families. While taking a lot of heat for not removing more people from the welfare rolls like every other human services director did, I found some vindication when the rest of the United States declined into a recession in early 2000. Many directors in other states called me and asked about our welfare plan and what they could learn from our experience. When jobs are hard to find and the unemployment rate goes up, so do the welfare rolls.

17 | Innovation and Change; Can Anyone Do This?

We now look at innovation and change. The first section reflects on changes that worked and others that didn't. Those that had the sustained support of external players were successful. The internal efforts were a different story. Chandler concludes that no matter how much energy was devoted to the cause, her efforts to change the basic structure just didn't succeed. Here we can feel her frustration with the wide range of institutional and organizational factors that must be aligned to make this now-popular endeavor of reform and reinvention successful. The questions that come up here are about what has to come together to enable significant change to occur, what skills are needed by organizational leaders, and what roles legislators and the public have to play to get the changes they desire.

While welfare reform initiatives were front and center at DHS—primarily because the federal government created a small window in which each state was required to make statutory and program changes—several other interesting initiatives were also being tried. Some were pretty easy; others were not.

Implementing a statewide electronic benefit transfer (EBT) debit card system to replace the food stamp paper-coupon system is an example of an easy change. The trick here was to join a six-state collaborative and fly on their coattails as they worked through the sticky implementation challenges. Joining a mainland *hui* meant that many decisions were made at 4 a.m. Hawai'i time, which corresponded to a reasonable meeting time in Colorado. I often made very important decisions in my pajamas on conference calls from home, happy that my mainland colleagues did not have videophones.

The long and hard-fought battle over child welfare reform is an example of a difficult, but successful change. A legislative initiative in Hawai'i laid out the challenge to totally reform the state's child protection system. This was a necessary and welcome initiative. Many community groups, advocates, staff, and the family court worked together to significantly improve the system. This occurred primarily due to their passion, consistent support, and perseverance. In this case, child welfare advocates and the public sector agencies worked together, and by finding strategies that were beneficial to all, the legislature responded with money for both the public sector and nonprofit organizations. Many beneficial and critical-needs services were expanded and improved. The lesson here is that nonprofit organizations, particularly those that receive funds from the state, could be powerful vocal supporters of DHS's budget at the legislature. Of course, there were also some advocate groups with a single mission or rights-oriented mission who often did not want to work collaboratively and preferred to fight for larger policy changes.

Program changes within DHS that required reorganization of its hierarchy and structure, even when incredible energy and perseverance were exerted, often didn't happen. The complexity of reorganizing units within a state agency—including the mandated amendments to the personnel rules, organizational charts, position descriptions, functional statements, and budget changes—all required a level of skill that very few people in the organization possessed or were motivated to learn. If the major players in the department personnel office—let alone those in B&F, DoAG, or DAGS—weren't one hundred percent on board, precious time slipped away and deadlines passed with no action taken. It was a daunting task to get and keep several offices, divisions, and departments involved in supporting the change and working hard on internal DHS reorganization. Each unit has its own internal issues taking up time, so effecting change at the department level often wasn't an important concern.

Here's a systemic change that illustrates what can be done with some good timing and a lot of persistence, despite the challenges. The innovation was called Family Group Decision-making and was a new way of providing services to families in CPS. By chance, on a trip to the mainland, I learned about a program that used new ways to engage and empower extended families in designing protective services for abused or neglected children. The program was originally designed by the Maori and implemented in New Zealand. It seemed like a perfect fit with Hawaiian and Asia-Pacific families. Queen Liliu'okalani Children's Center, a nonprofit private sector agency serving Native Hawaiians, was also interested in this approach and had begun training its staff in this innovative model. The staff at DHS, however, had some concerns initially. The staff's major worry was based on its interpretation of the federal and state confidentiality rules. Bringing extended family members, neighbors, and community people into a case conference was not a common practice in CPS. In fact, some staff felt it was illegal since the standard practice was to keep the names of abused children and their families confidential. Others worried that a more flexible meeting structure—meeting in relatives' homes, in parks, et cetera, and on the weekends or evenings—would be risky for case workers and would increase work demands.

My strategy was to build collaborations beyond the DHS organization while realizing that it is unwise to get too far ahead of where the staff is. I used some manipulation. I and a few staff members (called the bungee jumpers) planned a conference with the family court and many private sector agencies to discuss the idea of family conferencing. We pretended that there was a limit on the number of CPS staff who could come. The tradition at DHS was to mandate conference attendance to ensure that staff would be there. Coercive learning had been the staff development office's pattern, so restricting the number of people who could attend was novel. We established a requirement that anyone who wanted to come had to write, in twenty-five words or less, why he or she should be selected. This set up a buzz. We announced that only forty employees would be invited. In reality, we invited all the staff members who wrote anything. About two hundred employees attended. This was an excellent way to bring a new idea into an agency because staff curiosity was piqued.

After conducting several training sessions with the staff, we decided that the design of the innovative program would be to contract out to a private sector agency all of the actual conferencing activities. CPS workers maintained professional control over the referrals of families and, in concert with their supervisors, developed the policy that a worker could veto any agreements made in a conference if she or he felt a child would not be safe. This has happened only once in over six thousand conferences.

This program has been touted across the nation as an extremely successful child welfare reform initiative. Research and program evaluations have demonstrated that it is highly successful. In fact, a recent audit by the federal government noted that it was the most successful child welfare reform initiative in the state. The support of the family court, advocates, nonprofit sector, and courageous CPS workers made it happen.

Personnel Innovations; or, Maybe Not...

There is a delightful, and wise, satirical series produced by the British Broadcasting Corporation called Yes, Minister. *It is based on the doomed relationship between the politically appointed head of a ministry and his chief civil servant. The title reflects a common response to the minister's requests for action: "Yes, Minister" almost always was followed by ingeniously disguised inaction.*

Why do people in organizations resist change? Those of us who study organizations have asked that question many times. Some major responses include uncertainty about what it leads to, sadness at giving up what is familiar (even if disliked), loss of a feeling of competence, unhappiness about the change process, disagreement that change is needed, and concern that it will lead to additional work without additional compensation. And, of course, simple disagreement that the change is a good idea. If we start from the well-substantiated fact that even changes people like require adjusting to, then perhaps we can make some progress in making the changes that seem most important. Uncertainty about where the change will lead might be addressed by providing more information. The sense of loss might be met by deliberately building some of the organization's past into its future. Concern about feeling incompetent in relation to new responsibilities might be addressed by carefully designed training programs and by making it clear that mistakes are to be expected at the beginning.

But as Chandler points out, doing these things is no guarantee of success. Unions, personnel rules, or an uncooperative but key person can torpedo the effort, bringing it down with a thousand small cuts.

In Hawai'i, any state personnel action—change in position description, job task, office location—requires union consultation. While this is not veto power, the consultation can easily become a barrier to change, or at least slow its pace. Commonly, the union may ask fifty questions, some of which may need to be referred to the DHRD or to another state agency. Getting a response from an external department may take months. New job descriptions must be written for even the smallest job change, and this also takes time—months at best. Of course, DHRD has its own priorities, so the concerns at DHS are likely to sit in DHRD's inbox for quite a while.

The old story about the British civil service is true. In the British civil service, it seems that the timing for action is just never quite right. Eventually, with so many delays and inaction, the idea dies, or the minister (i.e., boss) leaves or gets fired. So why hurry?

In Hawai'i, it certainly must seem early on in a director's tenure that he or she doesn't know enough to even figure out *what* to change. Then when he or she begins to attempt change, obstacles emerge and the staff explains that the moment is not quite right. The staff suggestion is, "How about doing this in the next legislative session?" However, the

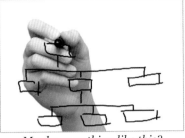

Maybe something like this?

next legislative session may have different committee chairs and even different legislators, so then the advice becomes, "Wait until they are more fully briefed about the agency's plans." That could take an entire legislative session. Soon, the director's term is over, and the change never gets to see the light of day. "Yes, Minister!"

This is not to label employees lazy. It does, however, describe a common phenomenon in which new initiatives often seem unnecessary to the staff, or perhaps foolish, and not worthy of the effort necessary to implement them. "Been there, tried that…," the staff seems to say. A person in a key position who isn't interested in effecting a change is usually able to delay the process or wear the requestor down so that nothing happens. On the other hand, planned change that is coming from the grass-roots level and is guided by a skilled administrator can move through the bureaucracy quickly. It can be done, but only when all of the stakeholders really want it done—a rare occurrence.

Staff members rarely want to move around within a department or even into another unit. Often, employees say that they prefer the devil (the supervisor) they know to the one they don't know and will not voluntarily move or take on new job tasks. This is true in Hawai'i even though union contracts give employees full benefits and seniority.

It is extremely difficult to reassign people within the state bureaucracy. A great deal of persuasion is needed to get a staff person deployed elsewhere. However, the deployment must be short term, and often the person deployed is not assigned to a department long enough to effect any significant change.

Employees often argue, for example, that things really are okay the way they are. However, the employee may fear that she or he does not have the skill set to successfully implement the change. Or the sunk costs of the

> 📄 *The attempt to reorganize the welfare program's eligibility workers units and merge them with units serving job finders was a frustrating failure. This One Stop Shop approach had been taken in most states and was clearly advantageous to a client entering the welfare system. However, due to the state's arcane job descriptions and an outdated position classification system, it proved impossible to move staff into new units with blended tasks. Even an agreed-upon pilot program never fully took off. Eventually, the delays lasted long enough to see me leave and the innovation never get implemented. (Yes, Minister!)*

training, equipment, manuals, et cetera may convince the employees that implementing the new change isn't worth it. Co-opting the unit leaders so they really see and believe that there are big benefits, both for themselves and their subordinates, is essential.

As Tom Wolfe wrote in *Radical Chic & Mau-Mauing the Flak Catchers*, the test is really who socializes the other first in bureaucracies. Clearly some significant changes took place during the Cayetano administration that improved services, lives of the consumers, and procedures for the employees at DHS. But there were many changes that stalled or faltered. The best result was achieved when there were people on the team who were enthusiastic about a change, had the skills to motivate others, and had the wherewithal (e.g., detailed understanding of administrative rules and regulations) to help make it happen.

There were successful projects that had staff members who weren't initially enthusiastic but were skilled in organizational change. They could design the necessary steps and could be inspired to work on implementing some new ideas as well as to inspire others. The worst-case scenario involved a skilled person who really didn't want to be involved in the change or see it happen. Sometimes it was possible to work around him or her. Other times, drastic measures like temporary reassignment to another unit could be taken. The biggest failure occurred when the skilled person had the support of other key staff and simply would not get on board. No amount of logic or persuasion seemed to matter. The best advice in this situation is to remember that not everything will come to pass, so it is important to pick and choose your important issues, develop a team of talented employees, and work hard.

Employee Culture; or, It's Good to Be an Anthropologist Too

Most employees aren't interested in obtaining power and the responsibility that goes along with it. This of course could be a reflection of human nature. Equally—or perhaps more likely—it is a reflection of the way conservative bureaucracies socialize the people who work in them. Would someone welcome additional supervisory tasks or take on more responsibility without a substantial pay increase? The problems could be more complex, and the stresses of the new role might outweigh its rewards. Employees might fear that trying to be innovative and showing initiative would create trouble in a rigid hierarchy. Or perhaps they might not be trained well enough to believe in their ability to take on these new roles and responsibilities.

The suggestion box at DHS got very few suggestions about things that employees could do to improve their work. Most were directed at what could or should be done by someone else or in some other agency. Few employees would make suggestions or research new ideas, apparently feeling apathetic or discouraged. The response to other employees' suggestions was often worry about what could go wrong if the change was implemented. Or an employee would express fears that he or she was going to get into trouble by proposing a new way of working. Employees certainly wouldn't have gotten into trouble with me for making a suggestion about anything, but they feared retribution nonetheless. Even young employees, the ones we'd expect to be the most bright eyed and bushy tailed, quickly became preoccupied with learning how the system worked and figuring out the informal rules for establishing good working and personal relationships. This is definitely the ingrained culture of many of the public sector agencies in Hawai'i.

Making Change in the Bureaucracy; or, Do I Really Have the Strength?

The most-likely-to-succeed approach to organizational change in private sector organizations has been the focus of a huge body of literature and an enormous consulting industry for many years now. A similar phenomenon has developed in the public sector in response to national and international calls for reform. As is the case for the private sector, recommendations vary except on one point: successful, sustainable, publicly responsible change is a big challenge.

It does not take much reading between the lines to detect some frustration in Chandler's conclusion that Nike has it right. You need to "Just do it" with regard to change in a public bureaucracy. Stated differently, the leader's role is to make change nonnegotiable: This is going to happen! Sometimes a crisis, such as a new federal mandate or a crimp in the budget, can help. Even though Chandler's experience suggests that consensus among the many parties affected is not likely and the decision must be forced on them from the top, there is still the need to create consensus and to reward those who support change.

At the end of this section, Chandler points to an incident in which a program that clearly would benefit needy clients while also saving taxpayer money was not implemented because constituent groups mounted protests. The fact that the groups seemed to misread the situation and misinterpret how their interests would be affected raises a challenging question. What should elected officials and knowledgeable administrators do when they have reason to believe they know how to serve a group's interests better than the group itself? There are competing dangers here. On the one hand, officials may simply accept the public misperception and not do something that is beneficial. This could be seen as forfeiting the responsibility to use their special knowledge to steward the public interest. On the other hand, the officials may be wrong, of course. Even if they aren't, citizens' views are expected to be taken seriously in a democratic system. There is nothing that stipulates public opinions have to be well-informed, or even rational, reflections of the interests of the people who hold them.

As already noted, incrementalism, or bit-by-bit reform, is usually the way most change takes place. Change forced by budget shortfalls or an external crisis is typically handled by an agency leaving most of its major programs and services intact and cutting funds equally across the board. Personally, I think Nike may have some things right. Sometimes you need to "Just do it!" Waiting for a consensus to develop among advocates, legislators, and agency staff rarely brings about change quickly enough inside a bureaucracy. To make significant change, there needs to be strong leadership with a consistent, persuasive message. Ideally, consensus builds around how this change is to be made, and responsiveness to it grows as the implementation plan emerges.

In order to make a big organizational change, there must be strong and consistent support from the governor, the legislature, the executive leader, the staff, and the community. All are necessary, and without at least two, a big change is not likely to succeed. Yet it is extremely difficult to get consensus on a new direction when the status quo has been meeting many people's needs for a long time. Dramatic change occurs when there is a new federal mandate (e.g., welfare reform) or a significant budget restriction that forces a reduction in a program or staff and a rethinking of agency tasks. Without those factors, change is maddeningly slow.

This is some heavy lifting!

Sometimes a tragic child abuse case, like that of Peter Boy Kema Jr., catches the attention of the press and the public. In this case, a child who had been under the state's protection was returned to his family, and several years later, he disappeared. While being blamed for losing a child is extremely difficult for the staff as well as the director, the press scrutiny probably helped shine a light on the state's child protection practices and the missing-children system, eventually leading to better collaboration between the police and DHS.

An example of how hard program reform may be is the state's Medicaid and Quality, Universal, Equity, Service, Transformative (QUEST) programs. Running the state's health insurance program for over 155,000 persons under a managed-care structure (QUEST) and 35,000 aged, blind, or disabled persons under a fee-for-service structure (Medicaid) was fraught with problems. The program is funded with a combination of federal Medicaid funds but administered through contracts with private health insurance companies in Hawai'i. Phase I of Hawai'i's Medicaid reform passed in 1993. It established a managed health-care system for all 155,000 eligible people. Each needed to choose a health plan and enroll as a member of QUEST. This was a significant change from the traditional fee-for-service system in which patients chose whomever they wanted as their medical-care provider. Any huge change in service would be difficult, but changing people's doctors and health-care plans is particularly complex. Nonetheless, it was done, and most believe the program has been a success. More people received health insurance coverage, and the cost increases declined at a faster rate than before.

I was interested in creating a Phase II that would enroll the Medicaid recipients (aged, blind, and disabled) into QUEST-like, managed-care plans. Similar programs had been created in Oregon, and the research had shown that managing the care of this very fragile and medically complex group was possible and beneficial, even though most consumers feared it. The change was designed to be incremental, but resistance was strong and broad based. The elderly and disabled were immediately opposed to anything that seemed to require a change in their medical system arrangements. Even though the plan could guarantee that most of them would remain with their providers, the constituent groups testified long, loudly, and hard at the legislature, raising the alarm that the change would be costly, difficult to implement, and inappropriate for Hawai'i. I hired facilitators from the university to listen to the community's concerns and personally attended over thirty meetings to discuss the change with concerned community members.

When some staff from DHS started expressing concerns about their own ability to launch such an innovative program, it became the perfect storm. If key agency staff don't believe in the change or are reluctant about the implementation, and there is vocal community opposition, the legislature often gets cold feet, even though millions of dollars will likely be saved. This particular reform didn't pass until 2009, well after I left office.

As DHS director, I felt the responsible thing was to implement Phase II and make changes that would contain the rapidly rising costs of health care. However, the program wasn't supported widely enough. Even replacing the Medicaid administrator did not move this initiative off the dime. Although it was a priority of the subsequent DHS director and Governor Lingle, it took sixteen years after Phase I was implemented to pass Phase II. It is possible that the idea was flawed. However, not implementing it, and making the budget cuts necessary to keep the old system in place, resulted in a reduction of the total number of persons eligible for Medicaid, a smaller benefits package, and a reduction in the reimbursement to providers. Instead of a program requiring elderly and disabled persons to enroll in managed-care programs, fewer people—both disabled and non-disabled—are now eligible for any kind of health insurance. We couldn't "Just do it!"

18 | Procuring Services; or, Hey, Didn't We Contract That Out?

📑 *Contrary to most people's perceptions, a huge portion of public services is provided by for-profit or nonprofit organizations. The situation in which another entity provides the services for which a public agency remains responsible is referred to as indirect government. In this section Chandler reflects on the challenges that come with the simplest form of indirect government: privatization, or giving to the private sector responsibilities that once belonged to the public sector. Historically, Americans prefer the use of the private sector to big government. This has long been a staple of electoral campaign rhetoric. Chandler's observations reinforce the view that, despite the extent to which indirect government is already woven into the fabric of American life, we continue to act as if government's inept bureaucrats are doing, or are trying to do, everything themselves. Chandler reflects on how much damage is done to public employees by this stereotype. She also comments on the challenge this stereotype presents to collaboratively designing systems that balance the efficient delivery of public programs with the inefficiencies that are inevitably associated with the requirements of due process, public accountability, and serving challenging unprofitable populations.*

The p-word (privatization) represents an interesting and complex phenomenon in the state of Hawai'i. While everyone in a public sector leadership position has probably read the 1992 book *Reinventing Government: How the Entrepreneurial Spirit Is Transforming the Public Sector*, by Osborne and Gaebler, and has bought into its simple message that government should be more like the private sector, the devil is definitely in the details. Replacing bureaucratic administration with entrepreneurial management and designating a single leader who is fully responsible and thus accountable were the popular mantras of the day. Yet contracting out services or tasks to the private sector, if those activities had been traditionally done by civil service workers, was not even legal in Hawai'i until quite recently.

The public sector unions have fiercely opposed privatizing almost any governmental function. The unions contend that the private sector will exploit workers and provide significantly fewer benefits while mishandling

Oh-oh, the P-word...

government contracts. They also contend that private sector firms come and go, put poorly trained staff on the job, and, when the job gets tough, terminate the contract, leaving even more problems for the public sector to clean up. This has indeed happened.

An expensive example comes to mind. The Medicaid program is extremely complex with multiple private sector health plans, a state-run eligibility system, and stringent federal rules and regulations. DHS contracted with a well-known information-system consulting company that had worked successfully in other states and with the federal government. While their credentials were impeccable, they were unable to do the job for the state of Hawai'i. Whether they didn't understand the specifications of the tasks or DHS didn't explain the requirements well enough, or they didn't bring in enough qualified staff to do the job properly, the contract terms were not met and costly delays ensued.

Another unfortunate example affected the state's Youth Correctional Facility. The facility had a long history of poor management, union grievances, lawsuits, and even cases of staff sexually abusing the incarcerated youth. A private sector contract was let to a well-known, well-respected, and family-serving nonprofit agency. The public sector union employees were not pleased with this and contended that DHS should just hire more staff so they could do their job more efficiently. The state agency was paying a large amount of overtime to the existing public sector staff due to high turnover, slow filling of vacancies, and an inordinate amount of sick leave being taken. Since there were mandated staffing levels, employees were required to stay on double shifts when other employees were out (or had quit). So a contract was designed for the private sector to take over both the security and counseling programs for the young women in the facility. Within weeks, it became clear that the contract as executed wasn't going to work. The nonprofit agency quickly assessed that it needed to hire more staff than originally planned for and admitted that it didn't have the proficiency needed to deal with this population. Within thirty days, it wanted out. This left the facility in an immediate crisis as the contractor desperately needed more staff. Ironically, it was the problem of not being able to hire sufficient staff internally for this facility that resulted in DHS's decision to privatize the job in the first place. Now the nonprofit agency recognized additional staffing was essential, and it was far more empathetic to the problems faced by the public sector.

Contracting out to the nonprofit sector for state and federal services has been done quite successfully in many human-service areas across the nation. Partnerships in the child welfare area have worked very well, and many reforms took place due to the innovations and flexibility of privatized service delivery. DHS is required to protect children from the threat of abuse or neglect, actual physical or sexual abuse and neglect, and psychological abuse and neglect. Very precise definitions of each of these terms are contained in the state statutes. There also are specifications that detail

---

The state is mandated to provide rehabilitative services for incarcerated youth in correctional facilities. There had been a lot of public and media criticism that the state's youth correctional officers were inadequately trained, took too much overtime, exploited worker-compensation benefits, and performed poorly on the job. A legislative briefing criticized the public agency's oversight of the facilities. In response, DHS tried to contract out the therapeutic component to a private sector agency. Problems quickly occurred. Within two months of awarding a contract to a private provider, the provider complained it couldn't meet the terms of the contract. Company representatives said they hadn't fully understood the nature of the situation at the correctional facility

and needed additional money to hire more and better-trained staff. The contract could not be modified and no additional funds could be added since that would be unfair to the other private sector bidders. Many of the DHS staff contended that if more money was to be given to provide these services, more state employees should have been hired or more pay should have been given to the existing staff. In this case, the provider chose to terminate the contract just two months after starting. A state agency in this situation has no options. Even though we didn't have sufficiently trained staff to do the job in the first place—the main reason for privatizing the tasks—the job and all of the responsibilities returned to DHS. The liability never wanes even if the contracts do.

exactly how much time is allowed to elapse before a report of child abuse or neglect must be investigated and sent to the court. Contracts were written requiring private agencies to meet these standards. There was sufficient competition in the community for these contracts, and the monitoring proved this to be a good relationship. However, in other areas, this was not the case.

Public agencies may neither pick and choose among those who receive services nor stop providing a service because it isn't cost effective. Public sector agencies assume *all* of the liability for any problem that may occur, and they remain the deep pocket in any lawsuit, even when the services have been contracted out to a private sector agency. This makes public sector employees nervous. The agencies are still legally responsible for tasks they thought had been delegated.

The longstanding constraint on privatizing services in Hawai'i was due to a statute that stated, "services traditionally provided by civil servants could not be privatized." UPW had filed lawsuits in circuit court asking the court to terminate specific private contracts. Honolulu Mayor Jeremy Harris publicly called the suits self-serving, saying the union's intent to use only public sector workers in the city would increase costs for taxpayers at a time when they could least afford it. The union filed the suits, citing a 1997 state supreme court decision against the use of private workers for services historically performed by civil servants. Justices, ruling on *Kono v. County of Hawai'i*, had found that privatizing was contrary to public policy. The mayor contended that the state legislature had passed a new law that allowed the government to privatize services as long as workers didn't lose their jobs as a result. The legislature later amended the law to permit privatization under a managed-competition arrangement. This meant that a state agency *could* contract out for a service if it could demonstrate that the private sector would do it at the same cost or less. Another constraint was an administrative rule that prohibited a private sector agency from being awarded a contract unless it had already been doing business in Hawai'i for at least one year—a classic catch-22. Under the managed-competition law, the private sector could now compete with the public sector to provide services. If awarded the contract, however, the private sector agency would be held to the contracted costs and not be permitted to adjust the contract under any circumstances. As the procurement rules eased, state agencies began developing more and varied requests for proposals. When a Republican governor followed the Cayetano administration, contracting out to the private sector burgeoned.

There seemed to be a strong belief that the private sector will *always* do the job cheaper, more quickly, and more professionally. However, if any trouble occurs while a private agency is managing a contract, all the liability and blame remain with the public agency since that state agency procured the contracted services. The state retains the responsibility for the contracted service but gives up a lot of authority to private contractors. When all goes well, the private sector gets the glory. When it goes bad, it is the public sector's fault for procuring that contractor's services!

So while McDonald's may easily hire and fire staff, change their product from hamburgers to *saimin*, continuously look at the bottom line, and quickly adapt to changing customer demands, in the public sector making these sorts of decisions is much more difficult to accomplish. In the private sector, competition keeps costs down. However, in the public sector with mandated services, involuntary customers, and civil servants with expertise in relatively narrow job descriptions and with seniority, there are numerous sunk costs and very little flexibility to make the rapid changes commonly seen in the business sector.

From this perspective, it is easy to understand why so many public sector employees seem to distrust and dislike the private sector. Public sector employees often are proud of the work they do and rightly feel slighted when the "Let's privatize it" mantra is heard over and over again in the press, at the legislature, and in the private sector itself. Contracting out services doesn't make sense to many public agency employees when the public sector already has the knowledge base, the skills, and the previous experience.

The issue of privatization needs to be discussed carefully. Many times staff members would agree that they simply could not do the additional work being mandated by new laws, programs, or procedures, and would welcome someone else taking on the work. However, when the talk was that the private sector was so much more efficient, cost-effective, flexible, and creative, et cetera, it irked many public sector workers. Bringing the staff into the discussion early and often is advisable. Public sector workers now have to write the contracts for the private sector and monitor the funds, staffing patterns, and the quality of the work. It is a good idea to have them understand the need for privatization as an alternative to work that cannot be done in the public sector rather than as a wish to get someone else (read as "better") to do the job.

This does not mean that contracting out for services is not an excellent strategy for public agencies to use when they need to provide additional or different services. The point is that just because it is a private agency does not mean that magic will occur. Government is responsible for solving many serious and complex problems, and cooperating with the private sector increases the chances for success.

Public Sector Efficiency Redux; or, If We Were Making Sneakers

The most common complaint about government is that it is not efficient or not as efficient as the private sector. While it is undoubtedly true that many public bureaucracies can make better use of their human and material resources, it is also the case that this inefficiency has a public value.

Chandler observes that government is inefficient because the legislature made it that way. She could as well have written that government is inefficient because Americans made it that way. The Founders of the American system did their work with an eye on the concentrations of unrestrained power they saw in European states. To avoid this, they created what we now refer to as checks and balances, an institutional design in which one part of the government can prevent another part from acting. The bottom line for this design is that it makes it much easier to stop action than to act. Another word for making it difficult to act is "inefficiency."

This inefficiency can be seen at the level of agencies where many constraints exist to prevent unchecked action. These include administrative rules, legislative oversight, watchdog agencies such as the ombudsman's office, and the right of cit-

How long have you been here?

izens to sue if they think an agency has not acted properly. All of these lead to caution and reduce the speed of action; that is, they are inefficient. It is useful, in reading Chandler's comments on inefficiency in the public sector, to think about the changes we are likely to accept to re-balance efficiency, responsiveness, and accountability, especially if it means reexamining concerns about the unrestrained power of government.

Efficiency and responsiveness are important public sector values. It is hard, perhaps impossible, to be both highly efficient and super responsive to the public's demands. An oft-repeated budget reduction and efficiency strategy in the public sector is to prevent a vacant position from being filled. Many times during the legislative session a legislator would make a recommendation to reduce staff through attrition. This may seem a quite reasonable request, but it really isn't. For example, if the Medicaid director resigned, should my department just not have one? Should the department be required to hire from within its ranks? And if you hire from within, then there is another vacancy somewhere else in the organization that might be crucial. If attrition would appropriately reduce the size of a bureaucracy in just the areas where personnel are no longer needed, that would be great. Unfortunately, the pattern of vacancies is not so kind.

The caseload among CPS workers was already higher than the national standard and the recommended ratios. Nationally, annual turnover was about fifteen percent. In Hawai'i it was actually lower than average, but nonetheless, if the caseload is 1:20 for a case management unit and the units each have on average three social workers, three social service aides, a clerk typist, and a supervisor, it matters where the vacancy is and who leaves. If a social worker leaves, the caseload will shoot up instantly to 1:40. If a clerk typist leaves, court reports may be tardy and fines may be imposed on the agency. So how do agencies meet their mandate of investigating child abuse and neglect when hiring is frozen? An interesting idea I heard from the staff was to freeze intakes and cap the caseload. The plan was to not take any more kids who were abused or neglected because the agency was in a hiring freeze! Of course this is impossible. The abuse doesn't stop just because the agency is poorly staffed.

An efficiency idea that DHS welfare eligibility office staff designed and was eventually adopted was to reduce the number of hours the welfare offices were open to the public in order to give the staff time to work on required case preparation and record keeping. In both organizational and staffing terms, this is a sensible idea because it increases efficiency. However, a legislator got wind of the change, took it to mean that the agency was reducing its availability or responsiveness to the public—which it was, at least in terms of client access—and the change was stopped. Eventually, with better information provided to the legislature and the community, this change did take place.

Public agencies are inefficient because the institutional structure within which they operate was designed to make them that way. This was for good, historic reasons going back to the founding of the nation. Merit-based recruitment and seniority were put in place to reduce cronyism and nepotism. In the private sector, if the cash flow is poor, a business can alter its hours or change the operation. In the public sector, business solutions just can't be easily applied and often don't fit at all, such as the unpopular furloughing of all state workers for several days from 2009 to 2011. Another particularly wicked problem is that in a welfare agency, as the economic times get hard and the tax revenues collected diminish, there is an uptick among the poor and needy requesting services. Thus, the workload for DHS staff increases while program and staff cuts are taking place.

19 | Lessons Learned

What does all of this add up to? In this section we pull together what seem to us to be important lessons from the reflections that make up this primer on organizational bureaucracy. We then share some thoughts on the prospects for improving public organizations.

Being Effective Requires First Listening, Then Leading It is important to understand the difference between programmatic improvements (what the public wants) and bureaucratic improvements (what the staff wants). It is crucial to listen to what the staff knows and where the staff wants to go. Agency policies and the organization of state government are extremely complex. There must an inclusive conversation among those who have detailed knowledge of the issues at hand. Nothing will happen if those who know how to make things happen are not on board. A colleague, Robbie Alm, refers to this approach as "pace and lead," meaning that you first must walk with a group before trying to change its direction. Energy is gold. Constructive persistence is essential. There can never be enough follow-up and follow-through at every level.

Supervisors Can Be Cheerleaders or Cogs in the Wheel We often are ambivalent about supervisors, those individuals who stand between the organization's formal leadership and the typical employee. Just as in the private sector, supervisors are crucial as both blockers and change agents. If a supervisor likes a program, the project, or the change to be made, it is much more likely to succeed, and vice versa. Supervisors are the key players in any organizational reform and can be cheerleaders or cogs in the wheel.

Perception Can Trump Performance Good management theories can work just as well in the public sector as in the private sector. The difference is that in the public sector, actions are usually under a public relations microscope. For example, a leader is perceived as first rate when positive outcomes take place (like when DHS was ranked number one in the nation on food stamp accuracy). You can be performing similar tasks and be perceived as an incompetent (like when the auditor found millions of dollars in apparent food stamp overpayments). How can this be? Sometimes the public gets interested in an issue regardless of the actual facts. Sometimes this works to the benefit of an agency and its leaders, and sometimes to its detriment.

Processes Need As Much Attention As Policies   A director could easily fill most of her or his time with administrative rules, lawsuits, mediations, the governor, and cabinet officials. However, the lifeblood of the agency is often not policy but its daily processes. From the perspective of the agency's mission, things like enough parking spaces, a malfunctioning computer, or inadequate air conditioning may seem minor. To employees who are charged with carrying out that mission on a day-to-day basis, such things matter. The lesson is that the director not only has to be tuned into these concerns but concerned enough to do something about them. This is essential for staff morale, for the smooth functioning of the entire organization, and, therefore, for carrying out the organization's mission. The challenge is for the director not to get dragged into employee concerns in a way that detracts from the agency's public purposes. Many of these issues can be delegated to managers at the branch and section levels but within limits. There are simply some things the director must tend to. The director's involvement may be necessary because the issue lies outside the manager's knowledge or authority, or because attending to the concerns reinforces the image of the director as a compassionate leader.

Internal Communication Is a Lifeblood   If there is a lifeblood of an organization, it is communication. The more often staff members get the information they need to do their job, and to understand where the agency is going, the better off everyone is. Unfortunately, while we all may say this, effective communication often does not happen. There are many reasons. Information is valuable, and power is often demonstrated by withholding it. The hierarchy restricts who can talk to whom, creating communication gaps between units. Cultural constraints may also play a role in reducing communication. And the challenge may be amplified in a public agency with privacy concerns. It is wise to make department-wide communication a priority from day one. Announcements that acknowledge someone's good work, a family event (a marriage, birth of a baby), or even a sports accomplishment and that are communicated broadly help the organization feel like a cohesive unit and a great place to work.

Without Effective PR, an Agency Won't Succeed   When poor communication exists among the agency leadership, the community, the media, and/or the clientele, the agency will not succeed. It is essential for an agency to publicize its activities and programs. If the agency does not report its accomplishments, no one else will. The most effective agency directors worked hard to get out an affirmative story each and every day. Some even planned television photo opportunities, like the Department of Land and Natural Resources (DLNR) director who would take the press to see how DLNR established and protected a sea-turtle preserve. Everyone looked great in the process. These types of opportunities were somewhat harder for DHS. Confidentiality rules prohibited photos of children being shown, and most clients felt stigmatized by being a social service recipient. Nonetheless, trying each week to publicize a story about a staff person's good works or a new beneficial agency policy, program, or accomplishment is always a very good idea. It also serves as an excellent morale booster for the employees.

Engaging the Community Is Essential   It is essential to ensure that the community gets into the agency and becomes a part of the policy development, program design, and implementation strategies. If such community partners feel left out, even good plans often go awry. As with staff, it is virtually impossible to provide too little access or give out too much information to consumers, providers, and interested citizens. Dialogue, dialogue, dialogue! There can never be too much dialogue even though this is an extremely time-consuming activity. Nonprofit organization advocates and citizens are extremely interested in what a public sector agency is planning to do and what its policies, procedures, and choices are. Perhaps the development of websites and agency ombudsmen will help some constituents learn more about the public sector. However, many agencies are not savvy about web technologies or do not have enough staff to effectively utilize them, so communication must be provided as a best practice (often in many languages) to make this work. There is common ground, but it must be cultivated.

You Cannot Give Enough Praise   It is not much of an overstatement to say that you can never give enough praise. People work for money, of course. But a huge body of research shows that money is not enough. We all like to be recognized and to feel that others appreciate what we do. It is commonplace to point out that in the private sector it is easier to reward individuals for their contributions. That is true if we are thinking only of monetary rewards. There is a long list of other kinds of acknowledgments that are meaningful to employees. For example, DHS instituted a *Mahalo-gram* process. Small yellow cards with the printed word *Mahalo-gram* on one side were distributed to the staff. 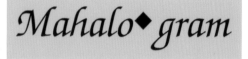 Staff could fill in names of colleagues and thank them for a job well done. We kept printing and printing them. People stuck them up all over their offices. One woman said that she took hers home and read them to her children at the dinner table. Money clearly is not the only incentive, and morale in a public agency can be easily increased with just a few sincere words of thanks.

In Organizational Change, Details Matter   It is essential to see the whole picture as well as small details in the big picture. Employees have tremendous concerns about their work and whether they can do their job well. They are keenly concerned about what a change will bring, what it will mean to them as individual employees, how it will affect their unit, and how it will affect the clients they serve. The good news here is that people in public organizations, like anywhere else, want to be competent. The bad news is that they can get stuck in their routines—what they know how to do—and not move on. The number of rules, administrative and other, that public organizations have to strictly follow, and that they must respect, probably contributes to lack of forward thinking. Whatever the cause, it is absolutely essential to provide sufficient and appropriate training so that staff members will feel confident to implement change and take responsibility for their new roles. Far from being a waste of taxpayers' money, focused training is a precious resource.

Success Is a Matter of Perspective   It is common to observe that success is in the eye of the beholder, but this is especially true for public agencies and their leaders. Success to the federal government is often defined as not making mistakes. To many state employees, success may be defined as always getting a reimbursement from the federal government. Success in clients' terms is often defined as when agency employees are responsive and generous. Clients are not interested in the employees' accuracy records. Success from an administrator's perspective may include developing creative solutions to problems, finding efficient methods, forming partnerships, or streamlining procedures. To a legislator, success may be resolving a problem by making a constituent happy. For taxpayers, success usually means doing whatever doesn't require raising taxes. For the media, success is a story that will get readers' attention—one we can assume is not about things going well.

It is easy to see that these different concepts of success can conflict with one another and that being successful in one way can easily be seen as failing from another perspective.

Recognize the Difference between Selling Out and Making Strategic Compromises Compromises are an inevitable part of work and of life. They don't necessarily represent a failure, and they sometimes represent significant improvements. Compromises are a reflection of the difference between ideals and reality, and without them nothing moves forward.

At the same time, there are issues worth standing strong for. It is easier, of course, to be moral, and do this if you have a secure job to return to, as Chandler did. She offered to resign twice. One offer was precipitated by a departmental budget shortfall and an angry governor demanding to know who specifically was responsible for underestimating the costs of the Medicaid program. She decided to protect a staff person who, in her mind, had done a good job and was not to blame for a less-than-perfect prediction in health-care costs. If anyone had to be held accountable, it was the director and not a budget analyst deep within the bureaucracy.

The second episode was over testimony on a bill introduced by the Senate designed to prevent a minor from having an abortion without her parents' consent. The administration's position was to support this bill in concept. Agencies are expected to testify in support of the governor's positions. Chandler, however, could not and called the governor to explain. Without a pause he said, "Then don't testify." What if she was asked for her position on the bill even without formal testimony? "Say what you believe." Chandler was surprised at how much respect there was for her personal opinion and expertise even in a highly political election-year setting. At the same time, the only way she learned this was by not compromising on her basic values.

The trick in all of this is to remain aware of the difference between selling out and making strategic compromises. An idealist never compromises. In a world with so many different and legitimate perspectives on complex issues, this person is quickly identified as someone who is hard to work with and therefore becomes ineffective. On the other side, a person who compromises all the time soon loses sight of the public purpose that brings her there in the first place. She is known as just a deal maker, a person without values.

In between these two extremes is the willingness to make bounded and strategic compromises without giving up on or losing sight of who you are and what you are trying to accomplish. What is called for has to be figured out in each situation; there is no formula here. The willingness to figure that out is critical to the integrity of a public leader.

20 | Final Thoughts

Many Americans express frustration, and sometimes anger, with public organizations. In the extreme this comes out as, "Bureaucracies! Who needs them? We'd be better off without!" To wrap up this inside look at a public bureaucracy we share our thoughts about these frustrations. We begin with questions that echo the unhappiness:

- Why didn't you (Chandler) force the issues and do more to improve things?

- Doesn't your experience prove that change is hopeless and big organizations just can't be improved?

- Isn't it clear that the answer is to run public agencies more like businesses?

- When people get into these public sector organizations, why do they seem to lose their minds?

Contrary to what these questions suggest about the hopelessness of government agencies, data show that Americans' personal experience is much more positive than their generalized opinions. In fact, in some cases it is more positive than their private sector experiences. (For a detailed analysis of relevant studies, see Charles Goodsell's book *The Case for Bureaucracy*, especially chapter two.) This disconnect is a good place to start in thinking about the issues these questions raise.

A number of explanations are possible. Maybe Americans don't like to be critical of the flesh-and-blood people they meet in agencies but express their real feelings when they can do so anonymously. Given the value of frankness and candor in mainstream American culture, that seems unlikely.

Another possibility is that individual experiences are indeed positive, but people are affected by stories they hear and incidents that are given notoriety in the media. This seems more plausible, especially the media aspect. There always seems to be space in the newspaper or on television news for stories that point to the absurd behavior of a public official or agency.

A more persuasive interpretation is that Americans usually have good individual experiences with public sector organizations but are prone to expressing dissatisfaction with government and bureaucracy because of a powerful inherited political culture. Early Americans accepted government only reluctantly or, as Gary Wills has put it, as a necessary evil. The nation's founding was animated by an emphatic rejection of the authority of the state and the church—two powerful interwoven institutions. Over the life of our country, being critical of and even vilifying public institutions has been seen as a way to protect freedom and democracy and prevent the emergence of an authoritarian government. In the context of that political culture, the criticisms are manifestations of a deeply felt, inherited skepticism as well as an embrace of individual freedom.

From a broader perspective, we can see that Americans share little of the view held in other nations: government and public bureaucracies, though not necessarily loved, are seen as a way to improve society. Governments that work can elicit patriotic pride. (A recent case in point is the reaction of British citizens to the repeated negative statements directed at their National Health Service [NHS] by American politicians in the health-reform debate. The criticisms elicited a defense of the NHS that reflected their national pride in it.) While Americans want many of the things that only government can provide, they are much more inclined not to want government itself. This allows them to have both good personal experiences (they obtain the service they want) and negative attitudes (government symbolizes something they don't like).

With that perspective in mind, we now can respond to the questions.

Why not force or mandate change?

The power of an executive director in the public sector, and even a CEO in the private sector, to bring about change by force or mandate is really quite limited. Or perhaps we should say that it is short lived. Yes, it is possible to fire staff who are unproductive or unresponsive or just incompetent. However, even Jack Walsh—the corporate leader who proudly says that when he ran General Electric, he turned over twenty percent of his staff each year—believes it is best if the employees themselves recognize they are not a good fit for the work that needs to be done. Leaving is much better than being fired. Public sector agencies in a small state like Hawai'i—and we expect elsewhere as well—do not have the capacity to fire and replace twenty percent of their workforce each year. The pool of trained workers does not exist, and the loss of staff knowledge would be disastrous. For this reason, it may be better to think in terms of moving the best staff to the executive team and to push for training and retraining employees who seem to be underperforming. Clarifying outcomes and expectations as well as encouraging employees to empower themselves and come up with ideas and suggestions for work improvements are better strategies than forcing an unpopular change and/or firing a recalcitrant worker. The public-administration literature is full of examples of hard-won but short-term gains. True organizational reform needs sustained support from all levels of the organization: top management, middle management, and the line workers. As one DHS employee said, pushing for change in a unit is like pushing hard against a plastic shower curtain. You can push and change the shape, but as soon as you let go, it snaps back to its original form.

Doesn't your experience in the public sector prove that change is hopeless and big organizations can't be improved?

Like lots of things in life, it depends on what you look at. We can notice the many program or service changes rather than fixating on the fewer internal organizational reforms. Designing a program change or contracting for new and different services is easier than reorganizing the units or structures of a state agency. But maybe the lesson here is that you can bring about change in a variety of ways. A focus only on the internal hierarchy limits the ability to do anything. Recent research on governing through networks (see O'Leary and Bingham, 2009) documents many new ways in which the public sector agencies can work creatively with private sector and community organizations to improve services in numerous organizational structures and relationships. Although we wish that the changes were easier and faster to accomplish, we don't see the struggles as hopeless.

Isn't it clear that the answer is to run the public sector agencies more like businesses?

It is an oversimplification to plop business strategies with their bottom-line mentality into a public sector agency that is responsible for abused children, elderly citizens, medically fragile persons, persons with a disability, or those who have lost their homes, jobs, and often their self-respect. The bottom line for the for-profit would be to move the disadvantaged and dispossessed to some other organization. For example, a health insurance agency would screen out the less fortunate since they often have pre-existing conditions or are likely to require expensive and extensive health care in the near future. Of course, and thankfully, this is impossible for a public sector agency, whose mission is to serve people who need assistance.

While some elements of a public organization may become more efficient, the core purpose of an agency like DHS is to serve, and serve responsively and responsibly. Our mission will conflict with the mechanisms that make efficiency the primary value in the private sector.

When people get into these public sector organizations, why do they seem to lose their minds?

Having the unfortunate experience of standing in line at a motor-vehicle office only to be told that you filled out the wrong piece of paper and that you must go to the back of the line or, worse yet, go home and return with the proper documents can make a person wonder about the abilities of the motor-vehicle staff. The public blames the agencies for making their staff sick or in need of an attitude adjustment when the rules and regulations designed to protect the customer—though he or she may not feel protected—are perhaps the problem.

Let's look at this another way. Perhaps the most frustrating experience these days is managing your cell-phone account. Highly competitive companies have outsourced customer-service jobs to India and Pakistan to find patient and charming people who must listen to irate customers all day. Their response, if you can make it through the phone call, is, "I'm sorry to hear that" or "That must be very frustrating" or "Have a nice day." The business model evidently works since the companies are quite profitable even though their customer-service ratings are extremely low. Perhaps, as has been the case with airlines whose passengers on occasion end up sitting on the tarmac for hours like prisoners, there will need to be government intervention for increased consumer protection! In part, people working in the public sector become frustrated, rude, annoyed, and unhelpful because they are unable to efficiently provide the services needed. Our experience is that people often go into public service with high expectations and a desire to improve the communities in which they live. We need more strategies and more public support to help them effectively and efficiently do the work they want to do.

Behind these questions, there also may be uncertainty about what it is appropriate to expect from public agencies. If our expectations are low, we are likely to be happier with our experience. If expectations are high, we are more likely to be disappointed. So where do our expectations come from? They seem to be strongly influenced by our ideas, though not necessarily the reality, about the private sector. In a business culture, the private sector is often viewed as responsive, efficient, flexible, and innovative. This is true even when that view does not comport with the time spent trying to get through phone calls, poor service, or misleading practices. We are generally more forgiving because the private sector is better aligned with our ideas of freedom and independence, and ready to believe things will be better if only government could be run like business.

Government organizations are not like businesses in another fundamental and also seemingly inevitable way: the places where conflicting public values are played out. Let's take the private sector practice of pay for performance. The idea is that the more value you produce for the organization, the more you get paid, which is an incentive to produce more, which leads to more rewards, and so forth. Pay for performance has been introduced into the public sector but with very mixed results. There are a number of reasons for this, but consider two of them. First, if employees can show that they are deserving of pay increases using agreed-upon criteria, requests to fund performance-based increases may come at a time when the legislature is simply unwilling or unable to comply, for reasons having nothing to do with the validity of the requests. To perform beyond expectations and not receive a pay raise has an understandably negative effect on morale. Second, the increased salary, however well deserved, may irritate some vocal legislators who see it as just another example of wasting taxpayers' money, a reaction even more likely in an election year. This has a negative effect on the agency's image. Here we are caught between adopting a private sector policy that values rewarding performance and letting democratically elected officials determine agency budgets.

The point here is not that we can't improve public agencies. Americans are well known for their pragmatism and problem-solving abilities. Arguing that the only solution is to reduce or eliminate public bureaucracies disparages that resourcefulness, implying that Americans are, for some reason, incapable of having effective public organizations. Are we wise to accept that claim, especially given the critical role these organizations are capable of playing in bettering our lives and our society?

In our view, the need is to better understand why public organizations function the way they do, including the rules and contradictory demands that we place on them. Government is us. The questions we need to be asking are not in the list found at the beginning of this chapter. Instead they are these: how do we become more realistic about what we are asking from government and the people who work in it, supportive in recognition of successes, and critical in ways that enhance accountability and lead to improvements?

On a Personal Note...

Writing this book has been a learning experience for both of us. Our perspectives changed as we moved between the efforts of scholars to understand public organizations, and the daily challenges, both large and petty, that people working in them face. We knew that being more efficient and effective, whether in a public or private organization, is easier to discuss, debate, and write about than actually do. We now are clearer that improvement depends on the relationships built between leaders and staff. Leaders need to have ideas about where they want the organization to go, but also must cultivate staff support and critical feedback. In this context, we highlighted the importance of supervisors as potential "bungee jumpers" or as blockers of organizational change. At the same time, we never directly addressed the issue of whether, as some believe, Hawai'i is "different" from the other forty-nine states in consequential ways. Its cultural diversity, unique host-culture influences, and distinctive island communities may produce differences in governance and the dynamics of organizations. In the end, we are left wondering how different things really are in the fiftieth state, and in what ways the uniqueness of our setting gives our public organizations advantages and disadvantages.

For Susan, being in a 24/7 public environment was a challenge quite unexpected—a kind she had not experienced. The press of the press was relentless at times, but support from friends, academic colleagues, and DHS staff helped tremendously. An important lesson for her is that while leaders can have big ideas and a big picture—along with policy-reform and organizational-change strategies—these will be reshaped by the organizational culture that exists (for a good reason). Many "details" are things that staff members feel deeply about. When? Where? How? Why? These are not impediments or stalling strategies. They are questions of crucial importance to those who will be responsible for the organization in the years to come.

Dick leaves this project no less committed to the work of improving public organizations. For him, the people most frustrated with an agency's shortcomings often are the ones working in it, caught between a public service mission about which they are passionate and the obstacles that drain their energy. The dialogue that produced this book underscored something he already knew: improvement is hard work. If anything, this dialogue increased his sense of the need to try. That means not being naïve about what is involved, and being smart about how and when positive change is possible. What we ask of government at all levels is just too important for us to do otherwise. He continues to see public service work as honorable, and distinctly different from business, and he is optimistic about its future.

We hope that this book will be of use to those now in public service, to those who are thinking about going into some form of it, and to those who may never have thought much about what their taxes are paying for. We hope too that sharing our perspectives brings light into the bureaucracies that, as Woody Allen said in another context, we can't seem to live with, or without.

References

Bowling, Cynthia J. and Wright, Deil S. 1998. Change and continuity in state administration: Administrative leadership across four decades. *Public Administration Review* 58(5): 429–444.

Brubaker, David. 2007. Where there's change, there's conflict (workshop presentation, University of Hawai'i, Honolulu, HI).

Brudney, Jeffrey L., Hebert, F. Ted and Wright, Deil S. 2000. From organizational values to organizational roles: Examining representative bureaucracy in state administration. *Journal of Public Administration Research and Theory* 10(2): 491–512.

Goodsell, Charles T. 2004. *The case for bureaucracy—A public administration polemic.* 4th ed. Washington, D.C.: CQ Press.

O'Leary, Rosemary and Bingham, Lisa B., eds. 2009. *The collaborative public manager: New ideas for the twenty-first century.* Washington, D.C.: Georgetown University Press.

Osborne, David and Gaebler, Ted. 1992. *Reinventing government: How the entrepreneurial spirit is transforming the public sector.* Reading, MA: Addison-Wesley.

Pratt, Richard with Smith, Zachary A. 2000. *Hawai'i politics and government: An American state in a Pacific world.* Lincoln: University of Nebraska Press.

Salamon, Lester M. and Elliott, Odus V. 2002. *The tools of government: A guide to new governance.* New York: Oxford University Press.

Tepper, Steven. 2004. Setting agendas and designing alternatives: Policymaking and the strategic role of meetings. *Review of Policy Research* 21(4): 523–542.

Wolfe, Tom. 1970. *Radical chic & mau-mauing the flak catchers.* New York: Farrar, Straus and Giroux.

Index